2610

British History in Perspective
General Editor: Jeremy Black

BRITISH POLITICS AND THE LABOUR QUESTION, 1868–1990

DAVID POWELL

MACMILLAN

First published 1992 by
THE MACMILLAN PRESS LTD
Houndmills, Basingstoke, Hampshire RG21 2XS
and London
Companies and representatives
throughout the world

ISBN 0–333–54849–3 hardcover
ISBN 0–333–54850–7 paperback

A catalogue record for this book is available
from the British Library

Copy-edited and typeset by Cairns Craig Editorial, Edinburgh

Printed in Hong Kong

Series Standing Order

If you would like to receive future titles in this series as they are
published, you can make use of our standing order facility. To
place a standing order please contact your bookseller or, in case
of difficulty, write to us at the address below with your name
and address and the name of the series. Please state with which
title you wish to begin your standing order. (If you live outside
the United Kingdom we may not have the rights in your area, in
which case we will forward your order to the publisher concerned.)

Customer Services Department, Macmillan Distribution Ltd.
Houndmills, Basingstoke, Hampshire, RG21 2XS, England.

CONTENTS

PREFACE

Twice in the 1970s – in February 1974 and May 1979 – British governments suffered electoral defeat in part at least because of their failure to maintain good relations with the trade unions and to prevent the spread of industrial unrest. Mrs Thatcher's government took office in 1979 pledged to curb the power of the unions once and for all. The erosion of union strength was to be one of the main legacies of the Thatcher years. Yet the events of the 1980s can properly be assessed only in a longer perspective. The 'Labour question' with which recent governments have had to deal was not the product of the 1970s, nor even of the period since 1945. It had its roots in the previous century and has been a constant factor in the calculations of governments from the days of Gladstone onwards. The purpose of this book is therefore to trace the emergence and analyse the nature of the Labour question as it has developed since the mid-nineteenth century and to assess its impact on British politics in that time. What follows is not intended either as a narrative history of the Labour party or an institutional study of trade unionism. The focus is rather on the relationship between the Labour movement and wider processes of political change, in particular the effect of Labour's rise on the structure of the party system, the conduct of industrial relations and the attitudes of government to questions of industrial reform and trade union law. In this way it is hoped to complement rather than duplicate the many excellent surveys of Labour politics which have already been written and to provide a brief yet coherent account of what is undoubtedly one of the most important strands in the political history of modern Britain.

In writing a study of this kind I have naturally had to draw on the original work of numerous other historians, and I can only express my thanks to those scholars whose ideas and research I have so shamelessly plundered. I am grateful to the editor of the series, Jeremy Black, and to the publishers for showing faith in the project at an early stage. My deepest debt of gratitude is to my wife, Pyrrha, for putting up with so much for so long.

INTRODUCTION
POLITICS AND THE
LABOUR QUESTION

In the first half of the nineteenth century labour questions impinged only intermittently and indirectly on political life. Parliament retreated from the more active policy of intervention over wages and conditions which it had sometimes adopted before 1800. The various Factory and Mines Acts of the 1830s and 1840s did set limits to the terms of labour of women and children, and the Poor Law reform of 1834 was concerned, at one level, with the operation of the labour market, but for the most part the evolving philosophy of *laissez faire* prevailed. Politicians were slow to respond constructively to the growth of trade unionism. The Combination Laws were repealed in 1824–5 after a successful campaign organised by Francis Place, but the unions obtained only a very ambiguous quasi-legal status. Trade unionism was seen by political economists and politicians alike as self-defeating and, in the words of the Whig Lord Melbourne, 'contradictory to the laws of nature'.[1] Labour protest was viewed as part of the more general problem of public order rather than as a political question in its own right. This attitude was reinforced by the nature of the electoral and representative system. Despite the radical campaigns of Chartism, working men did not have the right to vote (except in a very few cases) and were unable to secure election as MPs. They had some sympathisers and supporters in the House of Commons, yet, unless specific measures of reform were under discussion, labour questions remained distant from the central concerns

1

of an aristocratic elite whose primary desire was to preserve the substance of their authority against encroachment from below. To the extent that 'Labour' participated in this struggle – as during the campaign for the repeal of the Corn Laws – it was as the junior partner in an alliance of the industrious classes against aristocratic privilege.[2]

Between the 1860s and the 1920s – or, roughly, between the founding of the Trades Union Congress in 1868 and the formation of the first Labour government in 1924 – substantial changes took place. A system of aristocratic politics, in which domestic political debate centred largely on issues of a religious and constitutional nature, was replaced by a system of industrial politics, in which economic and social policy steadily assumed a more prominent role. The emergence of the Labour question was an integral part of the industrialisation of politics in the late nineteenth and early twentieth centuries. Governments became more closely involved in industrial affairs – in the regulation of conditions and hours of labour, the management of the labour market and the relief of unemployment, the provision of social welfare for industrial workers and even the monitoring and settlement of industrial disputes. The First World War gave a boost to state intervention in the broader aspects of the running of industry as well. At the same time, the growing strength of organised Labour meant that politicians had to find ways of relating the power of the trade unions to the other institutions of the industrial-political system and of defining the status and rights of the unions in such a way as to preserve a balance between the interests of the Labour movement and those of the community as a whole. The extension of the franchise and the eventual formation of a separate Labour party added a further, electoral, dimension to the Labour question as far as members of the Liberal and Conservative parties were concerned. After 1924, with Labour established as one of the two major parties of government, the industrialisation of politics seemed to be complete, although the Labour question was as much of a problem for the administrations of MacDonald, Attlee, Wilson and Callaghan as it had been for the Liberals before 1914, for Lloyd George between 1916 and 1922 or as it was for

Conservative governments from those of Baldwin in the 1920s to those of Heath and Thatcher in the 1970s and 1980s.

It is with this general process of industrialisation and with its specific political consequences that the present study is concerned. Within the overall framework of a chronological survey, three main underlying themes are examined. First an attempt is made to explore the changing role of government in the field of industrial reform, charting a course from the tentative interventionism of the late nineteenth century to the debates over nationalisation and privatisation of more recent times. Here, obviously, wider questions of economic policy and the social responsibilities of government are also relevant, so that the discussion of industrial policy provides a case study of the extension (and contraction?) of the functions of the state in modern Britain. A second theme is the rise of trade unionism and the institutional and political responses which that has elicited. Attention is focused particularly on the political dimension of industrial conflict, on controversies over the reform of trade union law and on the developing tripartite relationship between government, employers and unions which, according to some writers, has produced an increasingly 'corporatist' system of industrial relations. Finally there is the question of the impact of the Labour party on the pattern of British politics and of the extent to which the apparent institutionalisation of industrial conflict within the two-party system has affected the conduct of labour policy and exacerbated or accelerated Britain's economic and industrial decline.

In treating these themes, a study of the Labour question touches closely on at least two thriving areas of historical debate. The first of these is the controversy surrounding the decline of the Liberal party and its replacement by Labour as one of the two governing parties in the state. Among the questions to which consideration has to be given are the reasons for the emergence of a separate Labour party before 1914, the adequacy of the 'New Liberalism' of the Edwardian period as a long-term basis for progressive politics and the durability of Labour's post–1918 expansion when set against the problems experienced by the party since the collapse of the Attlee administration in 1951. By investigating the connection between the rise of the Labour party and the transition to a system of industrial politics, it is possible to show how the initial impetus to Labour's political growth derived from the position of the trade unions as a sectional interest which the Liberal party could not easily accommodate, but that this sectional strength was in turn insufficient as the base for a mass national party and ultimately became a source of difficulty, and even embarrassment, for Labour politicians when they sought to broaden their party's appeal. While the importance of the two world wars as a catalyst in British politics is discussed, an examination of governmental attitudes towards labour questions brings out the continuities between the 'Liberal' and 'Labour' eras rather than the reverse, with the Conservatives clearly the main beneficiaries of the changes which the process of industrialisation brought in its wake.

The other principal debate around which the study revolves concerns the evolution of the relationship between political parties, trade unions and the state and the nature and extent of trade union power. Just as the faltering of the Labour party and the Liberal–SDP revival of the 1980s reawakened an interest in the progressive politics of Edwardian Britain (building on the earlier work of historians such as Peter Clarke), so the problems of economic decline and industrial discontent in the 1960s and 1970s quickened academic interest in the history of industrial relations and the means by which governments had sought to placate and control organised Labour in earlier years. More recently, the alleged failure of a post-war consensus based on economic 'Butskellism', political bipartisanship and a habit of formalised government-union co-operation has stimulated widespread argument about the role of the state in relation to industry and the desirability of replacing a corporate, consensual, approach to economic policy with a more market-oriented one. The publication in 1979 of Keith Middlemas' *Politics in Industrial Society*, and his subsequent analysis of *Power, Competition and the State* since 1945 brought the study of these issues to the fore and opened up numerous lines of further enquiry, a process encouraged by the Thatcher reforms of the 1980s and the attempts to create a new dispensation for industrial politics in the 1990s and beyond.

In this context, perhaps a final word about the contemporary relevance of the material under discussion needs to be said. The emphasis of the present work is firmly historical. It attempts to explain how and why certain developments took place and to assess their significance in relation to one another. Its purpose is not to engage in political punditry, still less to make predictions for the future. Nevertheless, an element of topicality is plainly present. Commentators are now actively assessing the successes and failures of the Thatcher governments. As the Labour question takes on a more explicitly European dimension post-Maastricht, with pressures arising at home and abroad in favour of a reversion to more co-operative, interventionist policies of industrial management, a survey of the origins and demise of the corporate model of labour policy in Britain may be especially timely, even if space precludes any detailed international comparisons. Similarly, the changes that are occurring in the character and outlook of contemporary trade unionism can best be appreciated by comparing and contrasting them with the experiences of previous decades. With the twentieth century drawing to a close, it is sobering and instructive to be reminded that many of the issues of concern today – the poor performance of the economy, the problems of labour relations and the relief of unemployment – were being debated just as fiercely a hundred years ago and more. It is possible that in searching for patterns in the history of the Labour question since 1868 the student is left with the familiar feeling that 'Everything changes yet nothing changes'. But whether that is a criticism or a comfort it is not for the historian to judge.

1

THE EMERGENCE OF
THE LABOUR QUESTION,
1868–1906

The Mid-Victorian Settlement

Britain in the mid-nineteenth century was nearing its peak as a major world power. The industrial revolution and ultimate victory in the long series of wars against the French had provided the springboard to an economic and imperial supremacy which were the envy of other nations. Domestically, Britain seemed by the 1850s to have entered onto a period of equally enviable social and political stability after the unrest and near-revolution of earlier years. Of course, the picture of peace and prosperity can be overdrawn. In the 1850s, Britain went to war with Russia in the Crimea and had to suppress a mutiny among Sepoy troops in India. At home, poverty remained widespread and violence was still a ready means of mediating social discontent. The campaign for parliamentary reform culminated in the trampling down of the railings in Hyde Park by demonstrators in 1866. Yet, economically at least, the signs of progress were undeniable. Apart from the slump produced in the Lancashire cotton industry by the American civil war, the 1850s and 1860s were a boom period for industry and agriculture alike. Britain benefited from having a rapidly maturing industrial economy, with a well developed infrastructure, linked to a world-wide trading empire. By mid-century, the economy was less prone to the wild fluctuations that had marked the previous phase of its growth. Employment was more stable and there were increasing opportunities, particularly for the better-paid, skilled workers. For these 'aristocrats' of the labour force, the third quarter of the nineteenth century was certainly a period of social advance, both in the material and in the more general industrial and political sense.

The social and economic climate of the 1850s and 1860s was favourable to the institutional growth of the Labour movement. Trade unions had been developing in Britain since the eighteenth century. Despite the failure of the Owenite general unions in the 1830s, there had been a steady expansion of locally-based unions before 1850, notably in the mining industry. But it was with the foundation of the so-called 'new model' unions in the 1850s that trade unionism began to make an impact on the national scene.[1] The Amalgamated Society of Engineers, founded in 1851, had 12,000 members within a year and 21,000 by 1860. The Amalgamated Society of Carpenters and Joiners, formed in 1860 as a result of a dispute in the London building trades in 1859–60, quickly recruited 25,000 members. Although the new unions represented only a fraction of the workforce, they were able to sustain a permanent national organisation and to support full-time, paid officials. They also found that they were working more easily with the grain of public opinion. Whereas employers, politicians and political economists had previously been hostile to trade unionism because it challenged the freedom of management, threatened public order and ran counter to the principles of *laissez faire*, by the 1860s the prevailing orthodoxy was beginning to change. Employers were conceding the advantages of negotiating with organised rather than unorganised workers. Politicians had come to appreciate that the disciplinary effect of trade unionism could be a bulwark rather than a threat to public order. They were also keen to enlist working class support, with an eye to the further widening of the franchise. The economists, meanwhile, among them John Stuart Mill, had abandoned their theory of the 'wages fund' which had supposedly demonstrated that trade unions could not achieve permanent gains for their members since the amount of money in the economy available to pay wages was immutably fixed. Once this intellectual obstacle had been removed, and trade unionism had been accepted as a form of organised individualism, there was a corresponding recognition that it was in the interests of social stability for the claims of Labour to be met lest continued obstruction should drive hitherto moderate Labour leaders on to a more revolutionary political path.[2]

The process of accommodating Labour within the industrial and political system was nevertheless a gradual one and was not without friction. The extension of the franchise to some working men in the boroughs as a result of the 1867 Reform Act was an acknowledgement of working class respectability in the eyes of the politicians and an admission that working men had a role to play, in Gladstone's phrase, 'within the pale of the constitution'.[3] Since some, if not a majority, of the new voters were trade unionists, this gave Labour a potentially valuable leverage at the polls, if only they could find some means of exerting it. The failure of the three working men candidates who presented themselves to the voters at the 1868 election showed that this was easier said than done, however. Worse still, the unions had simultaneously to confront the threat to their position posed by the appointment in 1867 of a Royal Commission which, in the wake of the 'Sheffield outrages' of the previous year (where violent intimidation of non-unionists had culminated in the death of a man in a gunpowder attack for which union supporters were thought to be responsible), was likely to recommend further curbs on union activity. At a time when the case of Hornby v Close had shown that the courts would give no protection to union funds, the winning of the vote must have seemed small compensation for these setbacks on the industrial front.[4]

In fact, the Royal Commission of 1867–9 proved to be a turning point in trade union fortunes and paved the way for the mid-Victorian settlement of the trade union question. Three members of the Commission – Thomas Hughes, Frederic Harrison and the Earl of Lichfield – were sympathetic to the unions from the outset and published a minority report which recommended legal changes to strengthen the unions rather than weaken them. Even the majority of Commission members were impressed by the way in which the union leaders presented their case, and the final report of 1869 was in some measure a triumph for Robert Applegarth of the Carpenters and Joiners and the other members of what the Webbs later referred to as the 'Junta'[5] of secretaries of the Amalgamated Societies, who had been shrewdly advised by middle class allies like A. J. Mundella and the Commission member Frederic Harrison on the marshalling of evidence. The immediate upshot was that the Gladstone government, which had taken office in 1868, acted straight away to reverse the effects of the Hornby v Close decision, so giving the unions some redress against dishonest officials. They followed this with the more comprehensive Trade Union Act of 1871 which allowed trade unions to register as friendly societies to give themselves a definite status in law and afford further protection for their funds.

Even so, the Liberals did not give the unions all they wanted. The Trade Union Act was accompanied by a second measure, the Criminal Law Amendment Act, which sought to restrict the intimidation of non-unionists by declaring all forms of picketing illegal. The unions were also disappointed by the government's failure to introduce reforms of the Master and Servant laws, under which breach of contract by an employee could be considered a criminal offence. The imprisonment of stokers from the Beckton gas works under this legislation in 1872 highlighted the problem. Indeed, the Gladstone government found itself confronted by a Labour question of increasing complexity in the early 1870s. This was a period of rapid trade union expansion (for example among miners, railwaymen and agricultural labourers) and rising industrial unrest. The Labour movement was organising itself for a sustained campaign for the repeal of the Criminal Law Amendment Act and the reform of the Master and Servant laws. In 1868 the Trades Union Congress had met for the first time in Manchester as a forum to discuss issues of general concern to the Labour movement. Its 34

9

delegates nominally represented 118,000 trade unionists, but the powerful London-based unions, already organised in the London Trades Council, had held aloof.[6] By 1871 the London unionists had joined forces with the TUC and at its 1871 meeting a Parliamentary Committee was elected, under the secretaryship of George Howell, to lobby parliament on the unions' behalf. A related departure, born out of the failure of the working men candidates at the 1868 election, was the foundation in 1869 of the Labour Representation League which, with Henry Broadhurst, a former stonemason, as its organising secretary, was dedicated to securing the return of working men MPs to parliament at the earliest opportunity.

These developments did not indicate a complete breach between the Labour movement and the Liberal government. Liberals and trade unionists had co-operated widely in the 1860s in the campaign for parliamentary reform and in a variety of other radical agitations. Many working men looked with veneration upon Gladstone as an inspirational leader and a distinct philosophy of Lib-Labism had evolved which combined a specifically Labour perspective with the individualist, self-help voluntarism of the Liberal creed. Leading Liberals like A. J. Mundella, the Nottinghamshire hosiery manufacturer who became a Sheffield Liberal MP, involved themselves closely in the affairs of the Labour movement, pioneering industrial conciliation, helping with the formation of trade unions and joining the campaign for the repeal of the Criminal Law Amendment Act.[7] William Harcourt, who was to become Home Secretary and Chancellor of the Exchequer in Liberal governments in the 1880s, spoke out in support of the Beckton gas stokers imprisoned in 1872. There was, in short, a symbiotic relationship between the Liberal party and the Labour movement which temporary disagreements could not break. Significantly, the first two working men elected to parliament in 1874 – the miners Thomas Burt at Morpeth and Alexander Macdonald at Stafford – were both Lib-Labs, as were most of the other figures prominent in the Labour agitation of the 1870s such as Howell, Broadhurst (who became MP for Stoke in 1880) and the agricultural labourers' leader, Joseph Arch.

Nevertheless, the controversy over the Criminal Law Amendment Act did put Liberal-Labour relations under some strain. The TUC issued a series of 'test questions' to candidates at the 1874 election to see whether they favoured repeal of the Act and some Liberals accused the Labour Representation League, which ran 15 of its own candidates, of 'disorganising' the Liberal vote. It is possible that Labour disaffection was one factor in the Conservative victory at the polls. If this was the case, Labour was certainly well rewarded by the Tories for its support. After a short period of deliberation, Disraeli's government introduced the Conspiracy and Protection of Property Act in 1875 to modify the law of conspiracy and to legalise peaceful picketing. The Master and Servant laws were reformed by the Employer and Workmen Act of 1875, which made breach of contract a civil rather than a criminal offence. Other labour reforms enacted by Disraeli's ministry included a Factory Act and the Merchant Shipping Act, the latter being the result of a backbench initiative by Samuel Plimsoll.

Alexander Macdonald, one of the newly-elected working men MPs, claimed that in passing these measures, together with their other social reforms in housing and public health, the Conservatives had 'done more for the working classes in five years than the Liberals have in fifty'.[8] Yet perhaps the real message was that both parties, Liberals and Conservatives, had registered the importance of the Labour question and were anxious to conciliate Labour as far as was possible. Between 1867 and 1875 virtually all of the grievances of the trade unions had been redressed. The unions had been integrated on a permanent basis into the fabric of Victorian industrial life and they had made their first successful forays into the political sphere, where henceforth they were to be openly consulted by ministers on all the major industrial questions of the day. After 1875 they had few remaining demands to make of the party leaders. The enactment of an Employers' Liability Act by Gladstone's second government in 1880 put the finishing touches to the mid-Victorian settlement and testified to the restoration of good relations between the Liberals and the Labour movement, but by then the Labour question appeared, at least for the time being, to have been solved.

The Labour Question in the 1880s

The events of the ten years after 1880 showed that any celebrations of a final solution having been reached to the Labour question were premature. Indeed, from the middle of the 1880s labour questions became a more insistent and more permanent preoccupation of government than they had ever been before.

There were various reasons why the 1880s were such a pivotal decade. One was the mounting concern of employers' associations and chambers of commerce about the performance of the British economy in the face of competition from the second generation of industrial powers, led by Germany and the United States. The effects of the 'Great Depression', which produced a long-term fall in export prices during the final quarter of the nineteenth century, were beginning to be felt. Profit margins were being squeezed and there was a search for remedies. As early as 1881 a Fair Trade League was formed to press for the abandonment of Free Trade policies and the introduction of selective import tariffs to protect the home market. Measures to improve the efficiency of industry began to be discussed, including the adoption of new working practices and the training of a better educated workforce. Governments were obliged to take the warnings of incipient industrial decline seriously and to respond to pressures for remedial action. The 1889 Education Act allowed local authorities to levy an additional rate to provide for advanced technical education. In 1885, when a sudden downturn in foreign trade resulted in a severe economic slump, a Royal Commission was appointed to enquire into the causes of the depression in trade and industry.[9]

Concern about the economy was accompanied by concern about poverty.[10] Gloom was not omnipresent. Falling prices meant that for those in regular employment real wages increased by about 60 per cent between 1860 and 1900 and many sections of the working class experienced a steadily rising standard of living. But at a time when the slackening rate of economic growth was being acknowledged, evidence was forthcoming that even the boom of mid-century had not prevented the creation of a low-waged underclass of casual and sweated labour and the opening up of an ever-widening gap between rich and poor. The causes of the maldistribution of wealth were tackled squarely by the American social reformer Henry George in his book *Progress and Poverty* (published in 1879), which became a popular radical text in the 1880s. George sought the answer to poverty in a programme of land reform, but he was adamant that his analysis applied to industrial society and not just to rural areas.[11] The debate about poverty was given further impetus by the publication in 1883 of Andrew Mearns' pamphlet, *The Bitter Cry of Outcast London*. Its graphic account of conditions in parts of London's East End provoked an outcry in the press which attracted the attention of Queen Victoria and led, indirectly, to the appointment of a Royal Commission on the Housing of the Working Classes (of which the TUC's Henry Broadhurst was a member) and to the passing of the Housing of the Working Classes Act of 1885. Towards the end of the decade, Charles Booth's enquiry into *The Life and Labour of the People of London* (the first volume of which appeared in 1889) provided detailed evidence of the extent and causes of working class poverty, estimated to extend to as many as one-third of the capital's population.

Some of the problems of industrial society were addressed by an 'Industrial Remuneration Conference' presided over by the Liberal cabinet minister Sir Charles Dilke in London in January 1885. The conference brought together politicians, trade unionists and radicals of all persuasions for discussions 'on the present system whereby the products of industry are distributed between the various classes of the community and the means whereby that system should be improved'.[12] However, it was the high levels of unemployment generated by the depression of the mid-1880s that made the most immediate impression on the short-term economic debate. Previously the official assumption, embodied in the statutes of the Poor Law, had been that the failure of the able-bodied to find work was the result primarily of defects of individual character: shiftlessness, drunkenness, lack of exertion. In the practical experience of the industrial districts this view had long since been modified in the light of empirical contradiction, but it was not until the malfunctioning of the economy was more critically analysed by expert and academic opinion in the 1880s that 'unemployment' was established in the public mind as a systematic problem deriving from the cyclical nature of economic activity in certain trades.[13] Statistical returns from the trade unions and local authorities confirmed the extent of the problem and its political urgency was emphasised by the large-scale demonstrations of the unemployed that took place in London and many provincial cities during the slump of 1885–7. The demonstrations of 8 February 1886 in London had a particularly dramatic impact. A peaceful protest meeting in Trafalgar Square degenerated into what *The Times* described the following day as 'the most destructive riot within living memory'.[14] Property was attacked as a violent mob thundered through the streets of the West End, shattering the windows of the Carlton Club in scenes reminiscent of the Gordon riots of a century earlier.

Behind the fears of class war which these developments engendered lay the burgeoning power of organised Labour itself. The Reform and Redistribution Acts of 1884–5 had nearly doubled the size of the electorate, increasing it from 3 to 5.6 million, and had created a large number of single-member constituencies, in many of which working class voters were in a majority. Partly as a consequence of these changes, eleven Lib-Lab MPs were elected in 1885. They were mostly prominent figures in the trade union movement, notably Henry Broadhurst, the secretary of the TUC Parliamentary Committee since 1875, an MP in the 1880 parliament and, in 1886, the first working man to hold ministerial office when he became under-secretary at the Home Office in Gladstone's third ministry. Among his colleagues in the Lib-Lab group were George Howell, his predecessor as secretary of the Parliamentary Committee, and Joseph Arch of the National Union of Agricultural Labourers. The biggest share of Labour representation, though, was claimed by the miners, who benefited from the extension of the franchise to working men in the former county constituencies and from the geographical concentration of their electoral support. Six of the eleven Lib-Labs victorious at the 1885 election were miners, one being the South Wales miners' leader William Abraham (usually known by his bardic soubriquet of 'Mabon'), the others coming from the coalfields of Yorkshire, Northumberland and Durham.

The Lib-Lab successes were individual ones rather than the result of any co-ordinated strategy. But they came at a time when the Labour movement was entering on a new, and decisive, phase of its growth. The demonstrations of the unemployed – although sponsored by the Marxist-oriented Social Democratic Federation and not officially supported by the unions – signalled the adoption of a more assertive, even aggressive, approach to Labour agitation. In 1886, Tom Mann, a socialist, launched the Eight Hours League to campaign for the introduction of a statutory eight-hour working day as a means of reducing unemployment. The TUC endorsed the principle of the eight-hour day in 1890 and debated other measures of interventionist reform at its annual meetings in the second half of the 1880s. Once the worst of the mid-decade slump was over, these debates were conducted against a background of rapid trade union expansion. Existing unions recruited additional members more quickly than at any time since the early 1870s. Membership of the Amalgamated Society of Engineers increased from 53,740 in 1888 to 71,221 in 1891. This was also the period of the 'new unionism', which spread the benefits of trade unionism to hitherto unorganised groups of workers such as dockers, gasworkers and general labourers.[15] Provincial in its origins, the most famous victories of the new unionism occurred in London in 1888–9. The strike of the Bryant and May 'match girls', organised by Annie Besant in 1888, was a notable, if isolated, triumph for women's trade unionism. In 1889, Will Thorne's gasworkers and the London dockers, led by John Burns, Ben Tillett and Tom Mann, provided examples of successful strike action which were emulated throughout the country, albeit with diminishing returns, in places as diverse as Plymouth, Liverpool, Yorkshire and South Wales. The new unions never accounted for more than a minority of total union strength, but they symbolised, however briefly, the new mood in the Labour world. Altogether the membership of the trade unions increased from little more than 500,000 at the end of the 1870s to 800,000 by 1888 and 1.5 million by 1892. With an affiliated membership in excess of one million by 1891 the TUC was clearly re-established as a pressure group of considerable significance.

Industrial success in turn encouraged a more militant political stance. The Lib-Labs suffered a temporary setback at the election of 1886, when two of their number lost their seats amid the general collapse following the Liberal split over Irish Home Rule. At its 1886 meeting, therefore, the TUC set up a new Labour Electoral Committee (from 1887 the Labour Electoral Association) to replace the defunct Labour Representation League and to secure the election of more working men MPs. Most trade unionists were still content to work with the Liberal party to achieve their objectives, both for practical and ideological reasons. There was, however, some criticism of the Liberal alliance and of the obstructive attitude of the Lib-Lab 'old guard' on the Parliamentary Committee over issues such as the eight hour day for miners. The Lanarkshire miners' leader, James Keir Hardie, mounted an especially scathing attack on Broadhurst at the Swansea TUC in 1887, condemning his conservative and collaborationist outlook.[16] In the following year it was Keir Hardie who was at the heart of the first real challenge to the Liberal caucus when, after failing to gain the Liberal nomination for the Mid-Lanark by-election, he stood as an independent Labour candidate. His gesture was a forlorn one and he finished bottom of the poll in a three-way contest. The LEA and the TUC retained their basically Lib-Lab allegiance. But an independent Scottish Labour Party was formed (with Hardie among its leaders) in 1888 and already a number of other socialist and independent Labour groups such as the Social Democratic Federation (founded in 1884 from the earlier Democratic Federation of 1881) were coming into existence. Ideologically and organisationally they represented a challenge to the existing duopoly of the Liberal and Conservative parties and to the old order of leadership within the Labour movement, just as the growth of the Labour movement in the 1880s presented a challenge to the mid-Victorian settlement of the Labour question.

Politics and Industry before 1906

The emergence, or re-emergence, of the Labour question in the 1880s led to a significant shift in the axis of political debate. True, much time was still devoted to long-standing issues of controversy: Ireland, religion, the prerogatives of the aristocracy as landowners or members of the House of Lords. But alongside these staples of the old politics newer themes were claiming attention. Events such as the demonstrations of the unemployed or the London dock strike brought the problems of industrial society sharply into focus. According to the Liberal politician Herbert Samuel, the dock strike 'had drawn aside the curtain' to reveal the true facts about the conditions in which many members of the lower classes lived and worked.[17] In parliament and in the press the problems of industry were widely discussed. Considerable space was given over by newspapers and periodicals to the reporting of industrial disputes and to canvassing specific measures of labour reform.[18] Among experts, administrators and academics a similar reordering of priorities occurred, giving at least some substance to the claims of one writer in the 1890s that ' . . . from 1886 onwards, the Labour Question forced itself to the front and it is now the great question of the day'.[19]

The resulting debate ranged over a number of issues: the extension of protective legislation and the use of the power of the state to relieve unemployment and to carry out industrial and economic reform; the role of the state in regard to industrial relations and its proper position *vis-à-vis* the rival powers of employers and unions; the extent to which there should be overall political direction of the economy and the possibility of greater state intervention in the management and ownership of industry. Inevitably some of these areas were more contentious than others, and although by the early 1900s a more interventionist consensus was evolving there was not necessarily any firm agreement as to what the scope or purpose of that intervention should be. In this context it is important to appreciate that in responding to the complexities of the Labour question politicians were not simply deciding to what extent they should give in to the demands of the Labour movement. For one thing, those demands were not always clear cut. On some questions the Labour movement was itself divided. There were also countervailing pressures at work. A parliament which was composed overwhelmingly of the upper and middle classes, and in which many MPs had industrial and business interests, was concerned as much to control and contain the challenge of Labour as to appease it or add to its power. Ministers were guided for the most part by pragmatic and practical considerations, but they were influenced too by the inherited differences in philosophy and electoral outlook of the two major parties as they sought to come to terms with the consequences of Labour's rise.

Certain general trends operated irrespective of the party in power. The way in which the Factory Acts were extended by successive governments was a good example of the continuity of a tradition of administrative reform which had been developing momentum since the 1830s and 1840s. Conditions of work became more tightly controlled and inspection was made more rigorous. Asquith, when he was Home Secretary in the Liberal governments of 1892–5, instituted enquiries into the so-called 'dangerous trades' and appointed the first women factory inspectors. His Factory and Workshops Act of 1895 built upon earlier reforms introduced by the Disraeli and Salisbury governments and was in turn modified by the Conservatives in 1901, when the minimum age for factory work was raised to twelve.

A similarly cumulative process was at work in relation to the question of employers' liability to compensate their workers for accidents suffered in the course of their employment. Legislation on this issue was one of the main demands of the trade union movement from the 1870s onwards. The Liberals had responded to union pressure by introducing their Employers' Liability Act of 1880 and they attempted to strengthen its provisions with further legislation in 1893. On this occasion the House of Lords provoked controversy by blocking the Bill and insisting on the acceptance of an amendment allowing workers to 'contract out' of the provisions of the scheme. The Liberals withdrew the Bill to the accompaniment of mass demonstrations of protest sponsored by the TUC. An amended version of the measure was reintroduced by the Salisbury administration (under the influence of the Liberal Unionist, Joseph Chamberlain) and became the Workmen's Compensation Act of 1897.

These examples clearly demonstrate that industrial reform was often a hesitant, piecemeal process in which measures proposed by one party were amended and carried into affect by their ostensible political opponents. In the case of issues such as factory regulation and employers' liability, ministers were operating to a large extent as the executors of a policy devised by an expanding cadre of civil service and professional advisers rather than as the exponents of a partisan approach. The same cautious, step-by-step response was apparent in the handling of newer causes of concern such as unemployment. As has been seen, it was only in the 1880s that 'unemployment' became identified as an economic problem in its own right. The demonstrations of the unemployed in 1885–7, and the further high profile of organised Labour's campaign for relief and the 'Right to Work' during the depressions of trade in the 1890s and early 1900s (when statistics showed unemployment affecting 7.5 per cent of the trade union workforce at its peak in 1893 and 6.0 per cent of trade unionists in 1904),[20] made unemployment policy a key test of the willingness of governments to pursue a more interventionist programme of economic and industrial reform. Again, however, the response was gradualist, reflecting the conservatism of economic orthodoxy, and it was difficult to discern significant differences between the parties. The Liberal government of 1886 issued the 'Chamberlain circular'[21] advising local authorities to schedule public works for times of distress and the statistical bureau of the Board of Trade began to collect data on the extent of unemployment in particular occupations, but there was widespread scepticism about the ability of government to counteract the effects of unemployment by more vigorous action.[22] When the Liberals returned to office in 1892, the Chamberlain circular was reissued and there was some discussion of additional schemes of public works. The only other concession to Keir Hardie's lone campaign in the 1892 parliament as the 'Member for the Unemployed' was the appointment of a parliamentary select committee in 1895. Not until the Unemployed Workmen Act of 1905 was passed by the Conservatives did the state take a further initiative in the direction of providing help (other than the Poor Law) for the victims of recession.[23]

Yet if the handling of unemployment policy indicates the evolution of a consensus, there were other areas in which differences between the records of the governing parties could be detected. Although the Conservatives were in power for most of the twenty years from 1885 to 1905, in some respects it was the Liberals during their brief periods of office in 1886 and 1892–5 who were responsible for some of the most significant departures in labour policy.[24] For instance, it was the Liberal A. J. Mundella, President of the Board of Trade in 1886 and again from 1892 to 1894, who established a separate Labour Department at the Board of Trade, thereby creating the administrative machinery for collecting and collating industrial information as a necessary prelude to more effective intervention in the industrial sphere. Under its first 'Labour Commissioner', Hubert Llewellyn Smith, the Labour Department recruited an impressive team of civil servants, social investigators and trade unionists to carry out its tasks and it became an important factor in the formulation of government policy on labour questions.[25] Nor was this the only area in which the Liberals seemed more amenable to new ideas. The ministries of 1892–5 did their best to make the government a model employer by introducing the eight hour day into government workshops. They also experimented tentatively with the statutory limitation of hours which, together with unemployment, was the main test question of labour policy in the 1880s and 1890s. The Railway Servants Act of 1893 was the first piece of legislation to empower the government to limit the hours of labour of adult males (as opposed to those of women and children), thus setting a precedent that was capable of subsequent extension. A majority of Liberal MPs also supported the Eight Hours Bill for Mines sponsored by the Miners' Federation, although this did not become the official policy of either the Gladstone or Rosebery governments.

The same mixture of broad consensus and subtle differences was evident in attitudes towards governmental involvement in industrial relations. In framing the settlement of the 1870s, politicians had agreed that a voluntary system should prevail – that is, that parliament would establish a legal framework within which employers and unions could resolve their differences through negotiation and collective bargaining without the intervention of the state. In many industries, local conciliation machinery was created which enabled disputes to be settled by committees of employers and workers under the supervision of an independent chairman or arbitrator. By the late nineteenth century, however, there were signs that this system of conciliation was beginning to break down. The trend towards a larger scale of industrial organisation meant that disputes were taking on a national rather than a purely local character. The growth of new, more militant, unions, and the hardening attitude of employers intent on protecting their profit margins by cuts in wages and alterations in working practices, led to a more unsettled climate of industrial relations. There were a series of national industrial stoppages in the 1890s, such as those in the coal industry in 1893 and the engineering trades in 1897–8. The number of working days lost due to strikes or lock-outs rose to unprecedented levels.[26] Employers in industries like shipping and engineering formed federations to withstand what they saw as the threat of trade union power. In the courts there were controversial cases the results of which called into question the whole legal basis of the settlement of 1875. The case of Lyons v Wilkins (1896) raised doubts about the legality of certain forms of picketing, while the famous Taff Vale Judgement of 1901 – which required the Amalgamated Society of Railway Servants to pay heavy damages to the owners of the Taff Vale railway in South Wales to compensate for losses arising from a dispute – threatened completely to undermine the chances of unions conducting successful strike action.[27]

Although the extent of the polarisation that occurred should not be exaggerated, the deterioration of industrial relations in the 1890s highlighted some of the political problems that were to remain constant facets of the Labour question throughout the twentieth century. First there was the problem of the policing of industrial disputes. Through the Home Office and the local authorities the government had the ultimate responsibility for maintaining law and order and could thus easily be drawn into a confrontation with organised Labour if large numbers of police or troops were deployed during strikes or lock-outs. Inevitably the government was seen as taking the part of the employers against that of the unions, as in the dispute at Hull docks in 1893, when a gunboat was sent to the Humber, or during the coal stoppage of the same year, when the shooting of two miners by soldiers at Featherstone in Yorkshire became a *cause célèbre*, much to the embarrassment of Asquith, the Home Secretary.[28]

Secondly, as the increasing scale of disputes posed a greater and greater threat to the working of the national economy, politicians had to decide to what extent the government itself should intervene to effect or enforce a compromise between contending parties. There was even some discussion of the possibility of introducing compulsory arbitration, though on the whole this did not find favour with either employers or unions and was not recommended by the Royal Commission on Labour which reported in 1894. A third, related, question was whether, in the light of the legal battles of the 1890s, it was necessary to have a further reform of trade union law, either to modify the settlement of 1875 or to remove ambiguities from it. In each case the difficulties of reaching decisions were compounded by the fact that the government could not be entirely neutral, being an employer of growing importance in its own right, and by the electoral and party-political pressures that influenced the decision-making process.

As with other aspects of industrial reform, both parties contributed to the shaping of the governmental response, but again it was the Liberals who were in the van of new developments. In 1893 they set a precedent for successful ministerial intervention in an industrial dispute when the Foreign Secretary, Lord Rosebery, chaired the conference of mineowners and union representatives which brought to an end the six-month stoppage over proposed wage cuts in the coal industry. This was not the only example of industrial diplomacy by members of the cabinet while the Liberals were in power. They also attempted to create a legislative basis for intervention by introducing a Conciliation Bill designed to give the Board of Trade powers to undertake mediation in a dispute if invited to do so by the parties involved. A similar measure became law under the Conservatives in 1896, though there is some debate about how effective it proved.[29] Conservative ministers were much more reluctant than their Liberal counterparts to become embroiled in industrial negotiations. In any event, with the exception of the engineering lock-out of 1897–8, the level of industrial unrest subsided while the Conservatives were in office after 1895, partly because of the legal uncertainties raised by the judgements of the courts prior to and including Taff Vale. The officials of the Labour Department continued to collect data on industrial disputes, to publish their regular *Labour Gazette* and to offer their supposedly impartial services wherever these seemed likely to be of use, but, from a political point of view, the emphasis shifted to the question of trade union law. Even here, though, the Conservatives avoided a firm initiative, Balfour's government merely appointing a Royal Commission on Trade Disputes. The Liberals, meanwhile, despite reservations in some sections of the party, committed themselves to legislation to reverse the effects of the Taff Vale Judgement, if not to a complete restoration of the *status quo ante*.

There were other areas in which bipartisanship had its limits. Concern about the performance of the economy produced varying diagnoses of its ills and prescriptions for its revival. There were fervent individualists who clung to an unbridled free market philosophy, who wanted state intervention to be kept to a minimum and a strict low taxation regime to apply. Yet by the early 1900s the out-and-out opponents of intervention were working against the trend. There had been a big expansion of the public sector, particularly at local level, with 'municipal socialism' involving public control of utilities like gas and water. The placing of government contracts affected – some would say distorted – the normal operation of the free market and had an effect on wages and prices. The real debate was over how far public enterprise might be extended. For the Socialists, full collective ownership of 'the means of production, distribution and exchange' was the declared aim of policy, even if this had necessarily to be accepted as a distant dream. But there were sections of Liberal opinion too, on the 'New Liberal' wing of the party especially, where public ownership was seen as a progressive way forward, the state taking control of certain industries partly to promote greater efficiency but also to enable government to use the profits of enterprise to facilitate the redistribution of wealth.[30] Even those who did not want full public ownership of industry were ready to endorse state investment in infrastructural development and modernisation, possibly including the nationalisation of the canals and railways. Some measures of this kind were contained in a memorandum presented by Liberal industrialists to the party leader, Campbell-Bannerman, in 1904.[31] For the Conservatives, on the other hand, although there was much talk of the need for 'efficiency' (as there was from Liberal Imperialists like Lord Rosebery and Fabian Socialists such as the Webbs), the main panacea for ensuring economic revival was intervention of a different kind, namely the doctrine of Tariff Reform associated most prominently with the ideas of Joseph Chamberlain.

The differing response of the parties was explained partly by the different circumstances in which they held office, partly by other factors. The Liberals were more dependent on trade union and Labour support than were the Conservatives and were consequently more sensitive to the political implications of the Labour question. This did not mean that their policies were dictated solely by the desire to appease Labour. There was a solid representation of businessmen and industrialists in the Liberal party's ranks and Victorian Liberalism had always emphasised the desirability of co-operation between capital and labour in their own and the community's interests. The organicist reasoning of the 'New Liberalism' of the 1890s, which redefined the Liberal creed to embrace a more interventionist, regulatory role for the state, was similarly intended to maintain the balance between capital and labour upon which both the success of industry and the political health of the Liberal party were deemed alike to depend. But in order to build bridges it was necessary fully to understand labour problems and in some cases to offer redress. Gladstone, Rosebery and their successors in the party leadership were keen to adopt policies which would appeal to working class voters and consolidate the Liberal party's hold over Lib-Lab and trade union opinion without alienating middle class support. New Liberal writers like L. T. Hobhouse and J. A. Hobson made a detailed study of industrial and labour questions. Hobhouse's first book, which appeared in 1893, was on *The Labour Movement*. Hobson published a series of studies, including *The Evolution of Modern Capitalism* (1894) and *The Problem of the Unemployed* (1896).[32] The activities of industrialist MPs such as J. T. Brunner, a partner in the Brunner-Mond chemical firm and one of the signatories of the 1904 memorandum, ensured that the Labour question received close and critical attention from all sides.

The Conservatives, by contrast, were comparatively slow to identify the Labour question as a distinct political problem. The tradition of Disraelian paternalism bequeathed a legacy of interest in social questions and this was augmented by reforms proposed by Chamberlain and others in subsequent years. But the electoral imperatives which drove the Liberals to confront the Labour question were lacking in the Conservative case. There was no large reservoir of 'Con-Lab' opinion, except in the cotton districts of Lancashire and a few other areas.[33] When they were in power in the 1890s the Conservatives actually stood to gain from any splitting of the anti-Tory vote resulting from independent Labour candidatures. Only in the early 1900s, specifically after the loss of the Woolwich by-election to Labour in 1903, did this outlook begin to change. The introduction of the Unemployed Workmen Act of 1905 was a belated attempt to win Labour votes. Before that, the Conservatives had been content to construct for themselves a broad coalition of the propertied classes. Their appeal to the working classes was based on the slogans of patriotism and imperialism and vague promises of material prosperity. It is possible that they may even have benefited from the hostility to trade unionism exhibited by some sections of the electorate. Certainly the Conservative party's institutional sympathies were more likely to be with the employers' federations and the 'Free Labour' (i.e. non-union) associations than with the official trade unions, as Conservative support for the refusal of Lord Penrhyn to recognise the unions during the dispute in his North Wales slate quarries in 1900–3 confirmed.[34] While it would be wrong to claim that Liberal-Conservative divisions over the Labour question were absolute, since both parties clung to a 'centrist' position of sorts, there was thus a very real divide between them. It was mainly the Liberals' determination to prevent the estrangement of capital and labour which stood in the way of a more obvious industrialisation of the two-party system. Ironically, it was the same factor which led to the formation of a third party determined to champion the rights of Labour against the 'non-Labour' parties.

The Origins of the Labour Party

Until the mid-1880s, and indeed for some while afterwards, organised Labour conducted its political activities mainly in association with the Liberal party. What Professor Vincent has described as the 'habit of co-operation' had been acquired in the 1860s and was strengthened by the attachment of working men to the causes most closely identified with Gladstonian Liberalism: morality and national self-determination in foreign affairs; individual, educational and religious self-determination at home. The alliance was cemented by the growth of Lib-Labism and by the participation of Labour leaders like Howell, Burt, Broadhurst and 'Mabon' in an assortment of Liberal campaigns, from the Eastern Question agitation of the 1870s to the struggle for Welsh Disestablishment in the 1880s and 1890s. Gladstone and his colleagues did their best to integrate the Lib-Lab MPs into the framework of Liberal politics. 'Mabon' was presented with a silver leek to mark his first St David's Day in the House of Commons.[35] The appointment of Broadhurst in 1886 and Burt in 1892 to ministerial posts in Liberal governments, and the presence of no fewer than three successive secretaries of the TUC Parliamentary Committee (Howell, Broadhurst, and Charles Fenwick) on the Liberal benches in parliament, testified to the apparent warmth of Liberal-Labour relations on an institutional as well as a personal level.

Yet already by the 1880s, the Liberals' Labour alliance was under attack. Keir Hardie's candidature at Mid-Lanark in 1888 contributed to a breakaway which gathered momentum in the 1890s. At the election of 1892 three nominally independent Labour MPs were returned: Keir Hardie in West Ham South, John Burns at Battersea and Havelock Wilson, who became MP for Middlesborough. The last two co-operated in parliament with the Lib-Labs (in 1905 Burns took office as President of the Local Government Board in Campbell-Bannerman's government), but Hardie became a more and more outspoken critic of the Liberal party. In January 1893 he was one of the founders of the Independent Labour Party which was formed at a conference in Bradford attended by 120 delegates drawn mainly from socialist and independent Labour groups in Scotland and the North of England.[36] The ILP never achieved great electoral success. Its 28 candidates (Hardie included) were all defeated at the 1895 election and it did poorly at by-elections thereafter. It nevertheless represented a break with the older style of Lib-Labism insofar as its members were willing openly to confront Liberalism at the polls. In February 1900 the ILP joined with some of the unions affiliated to the TUC to set up a new Labour Representation Committee, with the

ILP-er Ramsay MacDonald as its secretary. Twenty-nine LRC candidates were successful at the general election of 1906 and they became the first elected representatives of the newly re-styled 'Labour Party'.

The causes and significance of these developments have been much debated. To link the formation of a separate Labour party to the spread of socialism is enticing but problematic. There were socialist organisations in Britain in the 1880s, the most famous being H. M. Hyndman's Social Democratic Federation, William Morris' Socialist League and the London-based discussion group, the Fabian Society.[37] Individual socialists played a part in the new unionist agitation of the late 1880s and early 1890s. The ILP adopted a socialist programme, its leaders – Keir Hardie, Philip Snowden, Bruce Glasier, Ramsay MacDonald – called themselves socialists and were undoubtedly influential in bringing a Labour party into existence. The fact remains that the Labour party of 1906 was not socialist in the sense of pursuing coherently socialist objectives or having an explicitly socialist political platform. From the beginning there was tension in its ranks between the socialist ILP-ers and the trade union MPs. The spread of socialism may have encouraged Labour to assert its independence, but the formation of a Labour party did not signal the wholesale conversion of the working classes or their representatives to socialism in any strict ideological or doctrinal meaning of the word.[38]

The decisive impulses behind the Labour party's emergence were practical and organisational rather than ideological. As the circumstances of the Mid-Lanark election suggest, there was dissatisfaction that Labour was not reaping a bigger political reward for its loyalty to the Liberal party. Labour had increased its electoral strength as a consequence of the Reform and Redistribution Acts of 1884–5 and the Liberals were more reliant on working class voters following the departure of the Liberal Unionists in the wake of the Home Rule split. Yet while Labour had supported Gladstone over Irish Home Rule and helped to sustain the Liberal party in its hour of need, local Liberal Associations were reluctant to reciprocate by selecting working men as parliamentary candidates with a view to adding to the nine Lib-Lab MPs returned in 1886. The Liberal chief whip, Arnold Morley, and the party's chief organiser, Francis Schnadhorst, attempted to remedy the situation, but although more than twenty Lib-Labs went to the polls in 1892 over half of them were defeated. In the course of the 1890s several more aspiring Labour politicians, including Ramsay MacDonald and Arthur Henderson, found themselves rejected as prospective candidates by middle class Liberal Associations. As Henry Pelling has commented, many of the early stalwarts of the ILP joined the party less because of a reasoned attachment to socialism than because of a desire to challenge the power of the Liberal caucuses and secure additional representation for Labour in parliament.[39]

Labour representation was of more than symbolic importance. The worsening industrial situation emphasised the need for political action to safeguard the legal position of the trade unions in the face of the employers' 'counterattack' on the shop floor and in the courts. Employers were already well represented in parliament; the unions had therefore to be likewise. By the end of the 1890s the Liberal party was no longer seen as being able to offer adequate protection for Labour's interests, even if it had wanted to do so. The Liberals had tried to pose as the 'friends of Labour' before their return to power in 1892, and with some success. But the ministries of 1892–5 had been a disappointment. Promised reforms like the Employers' Liability Bill and the payment of MPs had not been implemented. Little had been done to relieve unemployment or to secure the statutory regulation of hours. Conflict had also arisen because of the government's record of intervention in industrial disputes. Their willingness to send troops to areas where strikes were taking place, usually at the behest of magistrates who were themselves employers, was criticised even by some of the government's own supporters. Nor did it escape notice that a large number of the employers were Liberal in politics, some of them actually Members of Parliament. Coupled with the refusal of Liberal Associations to adopt more working men candidates – as in the Sheffield Attercliffe by-election in 1894 – these factors naturally strengthened the hand of the Liberals' critics in the Labour movement.

There was no immediate abandonment of the Liberal party by the country's trade unionists *en masse*. Lib-Labism underwent something of a revival, with three Lib-Lab candidates being successful at by-elections in 1897–8. The ILP conversely made no electoral progress and was engaged in lengthy but ultimately fruitless negotiations for fusion with the SDF. However, neither the brief resurgence of Lib-Lab fortunes nor the Liberals' defence of the unions during the engineering lock-out could reduce the underlying pressure for increased Labour representation. After the defeat of 1895 the Liberal party seemed to be in an advanced state of disintegration. Gladstone's retirement in 1894 precipitated a long and debilitating struggle in the higher echelons of the party which was not finally resolved until Campbell-Bannerman was selected as leader in 1899. Even then the South African War of 1899–1902 opened up fresh divisions between 'Liberal Imperialists' and 'pro-Boers' which reduced the party's effectiveness in parliament and sidelined its hopes of regaining power. The disintegration of the Liberal party coincided with a deepening crisis for the unions. The final verdict in the case of Lyons v Wilkins followed the defeat of the ASE in the engineering lock-out, the failure of the 1898 South Wales coal strike and the first phase of the Penrhyn quarries dispute. In 1898 the employers had formed their own Employers' Parliamentary Council to co-ordinate political action in defence of their interests. It was in a mood of considerable anxiety about the future, therefore, that at its annual meeting in 1899 the TUC passed a resolution agreeing to convene a special conference to consider ways of extending the representation of Labour in parliament. At the conference at the Memorial Hall in London in February 1900 the unions and the socialist societies duly established the LRC.

Again the significance of this act is open to different interpretations. Recently it has been fashionable to play down the extent of the organisational breach that opened up between the

Liberal party and Labour in the years before 1906 and to stress instead the essential unity of the Liberal-Labour 'Progressive alliance'.[40] This is an attractive thesis, more so than one which posits irreconcilable conflict based on socialism or class antagonisms. The LRC, it could be argued, was no different in kind from earlier Labour organisations which had worked with the Liberal party, such as the Labour Representation League or the Labour Electoral Association (both now defunct). Many of its trade union supporters were still Lib-Lab in outlook. Even most of its socialist members had begun their political careers as Liberals or had co-operated with Liberals, for example in the Progressive party on the London County Council or, as in the case of Ramsay MacDonald, in radical-socialist discussion groups like the Rainbow Circle. Labour men supported policies which in many instances were indistinguishable from those in the Liberal programme. Above all, the LRC enjoyed only a limited degree of independence. Its 29 victories in 1906 were achieved mainly through the secret electoral pact negotiated between Ramsay MacDonald and the Liberal chief whip, Herbert Gladstone in 1903, which gave Labour candidates a free run in seats where Liberals were unlikely to win in return for general Labour support for Liberal candidates elsewhere. The practical success of this strategy demonstrated that the Liberal-Labour alliance remained intact and that the political position of organised Labour was substantially unchanged from what it had been in earlier years.

Yet there is an alternative view to be put. The electoral pact enabled the Liberals to contain the challenge of Labour and to prevent a damaging proliferation of three-cornered contests, so improving the chances of a Liberal victory in the general election. But it was also a measure of Labour's increasing political strength. MacDonald had been able to negotiate the kind of deal that none of his Labour predecessors could have delivered. The LRC, even before 1906, was on the way to becoming a much more formidable organisation than either the LRL or the LEA, as the victory of its candidate, Arthur

Henderson, against Liberal and Conservative opposition in the Barnard Castle by-election in 1903 proved. It was committed, by decisions taken at its Newcastle conference in 1903 and the electoral agreement with the Liberals notwithstanding, to making its tenuous independence a more certain reality. It was resolved that its MPs would constitute a separate group in parliament and would refrain from taking the Liberal whip, something which the Liberals recognised as representing a 'vital change in the organization of parties'.[41]

Inevitably, too, the appearance of a larger, more independent Labour party in the Commons raised the stakes as far as the Labour question was concerned. It had become apparent in the 1890s that despite, or in some senses because of, the Liberals' search for new industrial policies, the differences between the Liberals and Labour were becoming more rather than less pronounced. Liberal protestations of the common interests of capital and labour rang increasingly hollow in the overcharged atmosphere of industrial confrontation. The New Liberals were in favour of collectivist reforms, but they were alarmed by the growth of Labour as a sectional interest.[42] In short, the philosophies of Liberalism and Labourism were increasingly at odds. The pact of 1903 effected a temporary rapprochement between the Liberal and Labour parties, but it did not preclude continuing disagreement over matters of policy, as the history of the Liberal governments of 1906–15 amply confirmed.

2
THE LIBERAL MINISTRIES AND LABOUR, 1906–15

At the general election of January 1906 the Liberals, having taken office in the previous December following the resignation of Balfour's government, won the greatest victory in their history, securing 399 seats to the Unionists' 156, giving them a majority over all the other parties combined of 128 seats in the new House of Commons. Although a number of factors contributed to the Liberal triumph – the Conservatives' unpopularity after ten years in power, hostility to the idea of Tariff Reform, Nonconformist religious revivalism buoyed up by opposition to the 1902 Education Act – its scale was attributable also to the smooth working of the pact with the LRC. Labour questions may not obviously have dominated the election campaign, but they undoubtedly influenced its outcome, and the Labour question in its various forms figured largely in the problems with which the Campbell-Bannerman and Asquith administrations had to deal.

Industrial relations and trade union law

The most pressing labour problem which the Liberal government faced was the reform of trade union law. The Taff Vale Judgement had left the unions in an exposed legal position which they were anxious to see redressed. This desire had accelerated the process of trade union affiliations to the LRC, which rose from 353,070 in 1901 to 847,315 in 1903, with only the miners (who already had their own MPs) among the big unions remaining aloof. At the 1906 election the reversal of the effects of Taff Vale came second only to the increase of Labour representation as an issue in LRC election addresses.[1] There was concern, too, that public opinion was becoming less sympathetic to the principle of trade unionism generally. Whereas at the time of the London dock strike in 1889 the unions had found the public mainly on their side, the success of the employers' counterattack in the 1890s suggested a hardening of feeling against the unions and what they represented. The individualist Liberty and Property Defence League supported the principle of 'Free Labour' and was hostile to any extension of trade union power. Employers like Lord Penrhyn and the majority of the railway companies (with the exception of the North Eastern) resolutely refused to recognise the unions for purposes of negotiation. In 1901–2 *The Times* published a series of articles which blamed the restrictive practices of the trade unions and their attitude of 'ca' canny' for what the paper called 'The Crisis of British Industry'. The trade unions hoped that the return of a Liberal government, stiffened by LRC support, would lead to a change in the climate of opinion and to the restitution of proper legal safeguards to end the regime of uncertainty under which union officials had been working post-Taff Vale.

The Royal Commission appointed by the Balfour government to consider these questions issued its report in February 1906. Its main recommendations were on the whole favourable to the unions. They included the reaffirmation of the legality of peaceful picketing and the granting to the unions of a corporate status which would give limited immunity from prosecution by allowing a distinction to be drawn between strike funds and the general benefit funds which the trade unions possessed. These recommendations were broadly in line with the thinking of the Liberal cabinet and were substantially embodied in the Trades Disputes Bill which the government introduced in

March 1906. The Bill ran into immediate opposition, however, from the Labour representatives. They considered its provisions too complex to be workable and feared that too many crucial decisions would be left in the hands of the courts, whose judges were presumed to have an anti-Labour bias. Instead the Labour party brought forward its own Bill, proposing a straightforward freedom from civil liability which gave the unions virtual immunity from prosecution for damages arising out of industrial disputes. To the surprise of his colleagues, Campbell-Bannerman announced that he intended to vote for the Labour Bill on its second reading and it was this measure which eventually passed into law as the Trades Disputes Act of 1906.[2]

Campbell-Bannerman's decision was politically expedient. He wanted to retain the goodwill of the Labour party and he was conscious that Liberal election propaganda had implied support for a full restoration of immunities, thereby laying the party open to charges of bad faith if they stuck stubbornly to their original scheme. It is possible that he did not realise the full implications of his actions, so complicated were the issues under discussion. Yet the consequences of the Liberal acceptance of the terms of the Labour Bill were far-reaching. The 1906 act did not simply restore the situation which the authors of the settlement of the 1870s had tried to create. It actually went much further than the legislation of 1875 by giving the trade unions complete immunity from civil action, in a sense placing them, as some critics argued, outside the law altogether.[3] This 'extra-legal' status was to be a source of controversy for most of the twentieth century, at least until the reforms introduced by the Thatcher governments after 1979. The Liberals' decision created more immediate difficulties as well, since it encouraged the belief that a Liberal government could be coerced by Labour pressure into departing from its position of considered impartiality and making concessions to Labour demands. By removing the unions from all fear of prosecution as a consequence of strike action it also set the scene for a further period of trade union expansion and escalating industrial unrest in the pre-war period.

To be fair, there were other reasons for the Labour upsurge and something of the sort would probably have happened anyway, even without the 1906 legislation.[4] The Edwardian period saw a steady rise in the cost of living, by four or five per cent between 1902 and 1908 and by a further nine per cent between 1909 and 1913.[5] Wage levels did not keep pace, but low levels of unemployment after 1910 (three per cent in 1911, 2.1 per cent in 1913) provided a promising context for trade union action. Discontent was particularly widespread in two of the country's main industries, the railways and coal mining, and in the docks. Rank-and-file dissatisfaction with the cautious tactics of union leaders produced added militancy and increased the number of unofficial strikes. The spread of syndicalist ideas (which saw industrial action as a political weapon) further heightened tension, although their appeal is difficult to gauge. Whatever the causes, trade union membership almost doubled, from 2.5 million in 1907 to 4,145,000 in 1914. Some of the increase was due to the implementation of government insurance schemes, for which the unions could act as approved societies, and there was additional recruitment in white-collar occupations and among women. But the traditional industrial categories still provided most of the big battalions and were the ones involved in the major disputes. The number of working days lost in stoppages topped ten million in 1908 and 1911, reaching an astronomic total of 40,890,000 in 1912. The number of individual stoppages also rose sharply, from 479 in 1906 to a peak of 1,459 in 1913.[6]

Strikes by key groups of workers like the railwaymen, miners or dockers showed how easy it was for strategically-placed trade unionists to bring the economy to a standstill. As unrest in these sectors became endemic, there were fears that the growing strife between capital and labour could make the country ungovernable, or that 'ransom' would have to be paid to restore industrial peace. The government's response to the unrest was twofold. The policies of conciliation which had been pursued in the 1890s were continued. Ministerial intervention remained a central feature, with Lloyd George, President of the Board of Trade from 1905 to 1908 and

Chancellor of the Exchequer from 1908 on, cast in the role of the cabinet's chief troubleshooter.[7] He achieved an early, dramatic, success in 1907 when he managed, with the help of the ASRS secretary Richard Bell, to avert a national rail strike by persuading employers and unions to agree to the establishment of Boards of Conciliation to which union members could be elected even though the railway companies still refused to grant the unions official recognition. In 1911, when the railwaymen did strike in protest at the slow progress made in setting up the new boards, Lloyd George again used his negotiating skills to secure a return to work, promising a Royal Commission which resulted in the remodelling of the Conciliation Boards so as to enable the workers to elect union officials as secretaries, thus giving the unions a form of *de facto* recognition.[8]

Conciliation was practised by permanent officials as well as by politicians. The Board of Trade had been given powers of intervention by the Conciliation Act of 1896 and its Labour Department had exercised these intermittently before 1906. After 1906 Sir George Askwith was appointed to the post of chief conciliator. He intervened with some success in the Belfast transport strike of 1907 and in the national docks strike of 1911. In 1911 he was given the title of Chief Industrial Commissioner and made chairman of the newly-created Industrial Council, a body which brought together trade unionists and employers to form a kind of industrial court of appeal which could advise or adjudicate in difficult cases. The formation of the Council fitted in well with the general Liberal belief (shared by the leaders of the Conservative opposition) in the need for means of finding common ground between the two sides of industry. Unfortunately it played no real part in resolving the unrest of 1911–13 (largely because it was by-passed by over-anxious ministers) and its meetings were suspended before the outbreak of the 1914–18 war. Askwith was left frustrated that he had not achieved more and later complained that the government had not followed a consistent labour policy.[9] At a lower level, though, the work of conciliation was carried on and the essence of a voluntary system of collective bargaining was preserved, with the number of conciliation boards in all sectors of industry rising from 162 in 1905 to 325 in 1913.

If conciliation failed, the government had to fall back on a combination of coercion and concession. This was especially the case in the tangled affairs of the coal industry, where miners and owners were locked in a series of bitter confrontations the roots of which pre-dated the stoppage of 1893. As the earlier dispute had shown, a steady production of coal was so vital to the national economy that no government could afford to stand aside from the industry's problems. The Liberals took a big step on the interventionist path in 1908 with the introduction of the Mines Eight Hours Act, which satisfied a long-standing demand of the Miners' Federation. However, the operation of the Act was far from trouble-free. In 1910 the Northumberland and Durham miners, who had always opposed statutory regulation of hours, went on strike against the implementation of its provisions. In South Wales a strike broke out over the rates paid for working 'abnormal places'. These disputes led to the large-scale deployment of troops and police reinforcements in the affected areas to prevent violence between strikers and imported blackleg labour. Troop movements had an intimidatory effect, yet neither in the mining districts nor during the dock strikes of 1911 and 1912 was the coercive potential of military force fully realised, largely for political reasons. In 1912, when the MFGB embarked on a national strike in pursuit of a minimum wage, the government was forced instead to offer fresh legislative concessions. A Bill was rushed through parliament to provide for the laying down of minimum wage rates on a district basis. This was not the national 'five and two' (five shillings a shift for men, two for boys) that the miners had wanted. But it was enough to persuade the union leaders to call off the strike and urge a return to work. Given that the coalowners had initially opposed the measure, it was a sign too that whereas the government could not overawe workers by the threat of military action they were prepared to use the power of parliament to coerce the employers.

Whether the actions of the Liberal government are interpreted as cowardice or a skilful avoidance of confrontation is partly a matter of choice. In practical terms their crisis diplomacy, with its range of expedients and improvisations, was reasonably successful and it allowed them to weather the storm. By the end of 1912 the worst of the pre-war industrial unrest was over. The call for a national dock strike in May 1912, during which Ben Tillett uttered his famous appeal to the Almighty to strike Lord Devonport, the chairman of the Port of London Authority, dead, met with a muted response. Lord Devonport survived and the employers vindicated their right to continue the use of non-union labour. The Dublin transport strike of 1913 had only a limited effect on mainland Britain. It is true that in 1914 the three most powerful unions – the MFGB, the railwaymen (organised since 1913 in the new National Union of Railwaymen) and the transport workers – formed a 'Triple Alliance' which seemed to foreshadow a fresh trial of strength with the employers and the government. But for the moment it was the Triple Alliance containing Germany and Austria-Hungary that presented by far the more serious danger. The Liberals had not found a lasting answer to the problem of labour unrest, and in some ways their action in passing the Trades Disputes Act and intervening to offer concessions to Labour had encouraged the unions to pursue a strategy of industrial brinkmanship. On the other hand, the unrest had been contained and no outright estrangement of capital and labour had taken place. The evolving system of collective bargaining was substantially intact and the rule of law had been preserved. For coping with unprecedented problems with industry and resource the Liberal ministers and their officials deserve some credit.

Industrial Reform and the Labour Market

In addition to confronting Labour's industrial challenge, the Liberal ministries of 1905–15 embarked upon a wideranging programme of social and industrial reform. A Workmen's Compensation Act and a School Meals Act in 1906 were followed in 1908 by the introduction of old age pensions and in subsequent years by a string of other notable measures.

The 'People's Budget' of 1909 confirmed the principle of redistributive taxation and established the use of the budget as an instrument of social policy. In 1911 the two parts of the National Insurance Act, dealing respectively with schemes of health and unemployment insurance, went some way towards laying the foundations of what later came to be called the welfare state.

The reforms were in part the practical expression of the ideas of the New Liberalism which had been evolving since the late 1880s. The older Gladstonianism was giving way to a more active, interventionist version of the Liberal creed. The New Liberals, stirred by revelations about the extent of poverty and alarmed by the growth of sectional, class-based politics, sought to pursue a policy which would unite all classes behind an organic programme of reform. Social legislation would bring material benefits to the working classes, but the redistribution of wealth would also provide a more general stimulus to economic activity. The middle classes, while having to contribute to welfare payments through higher taxation, would be rewarded by the security of a more harmonious social environment. This was the message which New Liberal publicists like Hobhouse and Hobson were preaching.[10] Their ideas were shared by rising young politicians such as Herbert Samuel and C. F. G. Masterman, both of whom became ministers in the pre-war governments. Within the cabinet, Asquith had long been an advocate of the use of the power of the state for the purpose of social reform, and he it was who was responsible for the old age pension scheme introduced in 1908. The other leading reformers were Lloyd George, author of the People's Budget and the prime mover in bringing to fruition the health insurance scheme of 1911, and the young Winston Churchill, who had joined the Liberals only in 1904 but who rose rapidly through their ranks to become President of the Board of Trade in 1908 and Home Secretary in 1910. Churchill wrote and spoke widely on social topics in these years, urging his colleagues to enter what he described as 'the untrodden field' of politics and outlining his thoughts in a formidable series of speeches and memoranda.[11]

A variety of other pressures were also at work. The 'official mind' of government, represented by the civil servants and advisers in the departments most intimately concerned with social and labour questions, played a significant part in shaping measures and determining priorities.[12] Ministers were heavily influenced by the arguments of the Efficiency school. Lloyd George and Churchill were both impressed by the economic advantages which Germany derived from its industrial welfare programme and indeed Churchill called for 'a big slice of Bismarckianism' to be introduced into British social policy. The philosophical niceties of the New Liberalism have to be seen against the backdrop of certain clear-cut social and political imperatives. Welfarism could be a strategy of social control as much as one of social reform, a means of humanising capitalism and reducing the economic grievances of the working classes. From a party point of view the Liberals were keen to demonstrate that spending initiatives could be financed under a Free Trade regime, so reducing the likelihood of increasing support for Unionist policies of Tariff Reform. They were of course acutely aware too of the increased threat which the Labour party could pose if a Liberal government neglected the work of social and industrial reform. As Lloyd George warned his fellow Liberals in 1906, if 'at the end of an average term of office . . . a Liberal Parliament had done nothing to cope seriously with the social condition of the people, to remove the national degradation of slums and widespread poverty and destitution in a land glittering with wealth . . . then would a real cry arise in the land for a new party, and many of us . . . would join in that cry'.[13]

The importance which the Liberals attached to the Labour question can be seen from the impressive range of industrial measures introduced during the lifetime of the Liberal ministries. Some of those affecting the conditions of labour have already been mentioned. The Mines Eight Hours Act of 1908 was a significant milestone on the interventionist road, being a more far-reaching and prescriptive piece of legislation than the Railway Servants Act of 1893. It showed, moreover, the willingness of the Liberal government to give precedence to the wishes of the trade unions over those of the employers, who were opposed to statutory regulation. Governmental interference in setting the terms of employment was further extended by the passage of the Minimum Wage Act for the coal industry in 1912, although a precedent of sorts had already been set by the Trade Boards Act of 1909. This last measure, which had been promoted for some years by the Liberal MP, Sir Charles Dilke, was finally enacted during Churchill's tenure of office at the Board of Trade and provided for the establishment, in a restricted number of the 'sweated trades' (principally in the tailoring and clothing industries), of committees with the power to determine minimum wage rates. These were occupations which were notoriously difficult for union organisation to penetrate, so that the Trade Boards were a substitute for collective bargaining rather than an extension of it, but there were some similarities to the machinery which resulted from the 1912 Act, even if, under the latter, the unions were more directly involved, on the model of the earlier 'sliding scale' committees.[14]

These three Acts do not exhaust the catalogue of legislation relating to the improvement of labour conditions. The 1906 Workmen's Compensation Act extended statutory protection for those injured in the course of their employment. A Shops Act passed in 1911 led to reductions in hours for those working in the retail trade. Lloyd George piloted a Merchant Shipping Act onto the statute book in 1906 which raised safety standards for merchant seamen, building on the provisions of the Plimsoll Act of 1876.

Unemployment was another labour question that, initially at least, was high on the political agenda. The Conservatives' Unemployed Workmen Act of 1905 had empowered local authorities to fund relief works from the rates and to form Distress Committees bringing together representatives of municipalities, Poor Law Boards and charity organisations. However, as unemployment rose again in the early years of the Liberal government's term of office there was renewed pressure for the central government to take more effective action. The Labour party proposed a 'Right to Work' Bill which would have obliged local councils to provide work for the unemployed.[15] Ministers were unwilling to accept this proposal (John Burns at the Local Government Board came in for particular criticism for his comparative inaction), but they did offer an alternative scheme of reform. The details owed much to the work of William Beveridge, a recent recruit to the staff of the Board of Trade whose study, *Unemployment, a Problem of Industry*, was published in 1909.[16] He was the latest in a long line of reformers, J. A. Hobson among them, to point to the systematic causes of unemployment and to identify its cyclical nature in certain basic industries. The remedy he advocated, and which the government, in the person of Winston Churchill, adopted, had two main features. First, in 1909, there was introduced the Labour Exchanges Act, intended to establish a system of 'industrial intelligence' which would provide the government, via the Board of Trade, with information about the labour market while at the same time providing means of putting employers in touch with men genuinely seeking work. The 1909 Act was less sweeping than Beveridge had originally envisaged. Exchanges were not opened throughout the country and registration of the unemployed was made voluntary not compulsory, in deference to trade union objections. But the measure was the first real attempt to bring about an efficient rationalisation of the labour market rather than relying just on the palliatives of public works.

The second stage of the attack on unemployment was the scheme of unemployment insurance, introduced as Part II of the National Insurance Act of 1911. Again the early ministerial impetus came from Churchill, although he had moved on to the Home Office (and then the Admiralty) before the legislation was fully implemented. Despite criticism of its limitations, for its time the Liberal plan was a bold and imaginative one. It covered some two and a quarter million workers, mainly in the building, engineering and shipbuilding industries, who were likely to suffer temporary unemployment due to trade depression. In return for a weekly insurance contribution, supplemented by employers and the state, workers were guaranteed a payment of seven shillings per week (for a maximum of fifteen weeks) in any period when they were out of work. The sums were small, but the recognition by the government of the need for assistance outside the penal confines of the Poor Law was important. Coupled with the health insurance schemes masterminded by Lloyd George and his advisers, the unemployment measures provided a framework for the future extension of state welfare provision and offered a system of welfare support to the industrial workforce which marked a considerable advance on previous practice.

There were cautious advances, too, in other areas of economic and industrial policy. The government did not pursue some of the more adventurous suggestions of the 1904 Brunner memorandum, such as the nationalisation of the waterways, and they were more reluctant in practice than in theory to infringe the rights of private property.[17] On the other hand, some measures were taken to stimulate industrial reorganisation and to promote greater economic efficiency. Lloyd George's term at the Board of Trade from 1905 to 1908 saw a number of initiatives, including the decision to undertake the first census of industrial production.[18] Lloyd George also carried through a reorganisation of the London docks by creating the Port of London Authority. Another measure of importance was the Patents Act. The Development Act which accompanied the 1909 budget provided £12 million of government funds to finance selected job-creating public works, another instance of the Liberals' readiness to experiment with ways of improving the functioning of the economy, both to provide employment and to raise the level of national economic competitiveness.

It would be wrong to view the Liberal measures as narrowly partisan, either in conception or detail. True, the 1909 budget targeted landowners and landlords, as did Lloyd George's land reform plans of 1912–14.[19] But many of the industrial measures were welcomed and supported by the Conservative opposition. Moreover, they were undertaken only after wide consultations with employers, trade unions and other interested parties. In that sense they represented a compromise or consensus approach. Indeed, in the immediate pre-war years the Conservatives were evincing a much greater interest in industrial and labour questions on their own account. For many Conservatives, including the party's leader after 1911, Andrew Bonar Law, Tariff Reform remained a long-term objective and was the policy best suited to securing industrial prosperity and a higher standard of living. In the interim, however, they were prepared to consider other ways of ameliorating social conditions. A Unionist Social Reform Committee was formed, attracting figures as diverse as F. E. Smith and Stanley Baldwin. Conservative politicians joined their Liberal counterparts in stressing the need for harmony in industrial relations, moderation in dealing with the trade unions and selective action by the state to relieve the burdens of the wage-earning classes.[20]

The effectiveness of the Liberal reforms is difficult to judge. Their intentions were limited. They were not designed to alter the fundamental structure of capitalism or to eradicate the immense problems of poverty that still plagued Edwardian society. Yet even their more modest aims were only partially achieved. The insurance schemes were hardly fully operational before the outbreak of war in 1914 and therefore cannot be evaluated objectively. Even so, it is clear that they were not over-popular with their consumers.[21] There was resentment from workers who disliked being forced to make compulsory contributions for no immediate reward. The trade unions, who feared that their own benefit functions were being usurped, were only persuaded into acquiescence by being allowed to register as approved societies under the Act. Similarly, neither the minimum wage legislation nor the introduction of labour exchanges was universally welcome, the latter being viewed with particular suspicion by the unions who were worried that the system might be used by employers to recruit non-union labour. The policies subsumed under the label of the New Liberalism may thus have been a coherent attempt to deal with the variegated problems of industrial society. More likely they were a piecemeal response to particular facets of the Labour question. But in any event they contained a cruel paradox. They showed that Liberal politicians were developing more managerial techniques and that they were prepared to extend the apparatus and responsibilities of the state in regard to the industrial system. However, far from quietening social unrest and leading to a closer relationship between the Liberals and Labour, in some ways they had the reverse effect. In trying to meet Labour's legitimate demands while adopting policies which could be justified to their own supporters the Liberals actually provoked conflict with the very groups their measures were intended to pacify. They also raised expectations of further reforms which they could not immediately satisfy. The Liberal social reforms were an honest attempt to deal with the welfare problems of the Labour question, to smooth the operation of the labour market and to promote greater industrial efficiency. But, given the constraints of the government's position and the economic circumstances of the time, the feeling persists that, as a strategy for appeasing Labour, they were doomed to failure.

Liberalism, Labour and the Progressive Alliance

The 1906 election confirmed the arrival of the Labour party as a serious political force, yet its success was conditional upon Liberal support. Consequently there are two broadly differing views of the way in which the Liberal-Labour relationship developed between 1906 and 1914. One sees a further strengthening of the 'Progressive alliance' taking place, based on continued co-operation during the elections of 1910 and the growing hold of New Liberal ideas over the Liberal party which led to the adoption of social reformist policies similar to those which Labour itself was advocating. By 1914, according to this scenario, the transition to a more class-based system of electoral politics had been made and the progressive alliance was still in good shape. Against this, it is possible to stress the points of difference between the Liberal and Labour parties rather than the common ground. Having achieved its electoral breakthrough in 1906, Labour was fast establishing a separate identity for itself as a focus for working class votes. It was not afraid to challenge the policies of the Liberal government and it was developing an independent organisational base which gave it the capacity to break free from the confines of the progressive alliance if it chose to do so. When the war broke out in 1914, it was still unclear as to whether the Liberals and Labour would be allies or opponents in the next general election.[22]

In order to assess the political impact of the Labour question it is necessary to explore these arguments in more detail. How far did the Edwardian Labour party occupy a separate niche within the political system and what were its prospects for future expansion? The early omens were certainly good. Although it did not hold the balance of power in parliament and was overshadowed by the large Liberal majority, the Labour party managed to secure some early legislative successes, the most noteworthy being the Trades Disputes Act of 1906. In 1907 two by-elections were won at the Liberals' expense at Jarrow and Colne Valley (though the victory in the latter of the independent socialist Victor Grayson was an embarrassment for the official Labour leadership). These victories were followed in 1908 by the decision of the Miners' Federation to affiliate to the Labour party, a move which led to the virtual extinction of the parliamentary Lib-Lab group. Yet there were setbacks as well. Keir Hardie proved to be an ineffective chairman of the Labour party in the Commons during the first two sessions of the new parliament (he was succeeded by Arthur Henderson in 1908), and there was dissension between trade unionist and socialist MPs. Apart from the passage of the Mines Eight Hours Act in 1908, the early successes in the legislative sphere were not repeated. Most seriously, the decision of the House of Lords in the 1909 Osborne case threatened the financial base of the party, awarding a judgement in favour of W. V. Osborne of the ASRS, who had sought an injunction to prevent union contributions to Labour funds without the consent of the membership. If this judgement could not be reversed the whole future of a Labour party based on trade union support was plunged into doubt.

The crisis in Labour's fortunes coincided with the climax of the conflict between the Liberal government and the House of Lords. Despite their overwhelming Commons majority, the Liberals had been hamstrung since 1906 by the Conservative dominance of the Upper House. A number of Liberal Bills had been amended or rejected by the Conservative peers. In November 1909, the Lords took the ultimate step of rejecting Lloyd George's budget on the grounds that its proposals for a super tax and a national land valuation were class legislation in the guise of a finance Bill. Asquith immediately sought a dissolution, and in January 1910 a general election was held in an attempt to resolve the question of who should rule, 'the peers or the people'? An inconclusive result (the Liberals won 274 seats to the Unionists' 272) led to a further general election in December, which was also inconclusive. The Liberal government remained in power with Irish Nationalist support, however, and duly carried the Parliament Act of 1911, removing the veto of the House of Lords and replacing the Septennial Act with a maximum five-year period between general elections.

The constitutional crisis of 1909–11 gave the Liberals the chance to recapture the political initiative, which they had been in danger of losing, and threatened the Labour party with marginalisation. Not only did the 'peers versus people' aspect of the 1910 elections reawaken the traditional Liberal radicalism of the aristocratic political era. The new emphasis on social reform in the Liberal programme, to be financed through progressive taxation, enabled the Liberals to steal the limelight from the Labour critics of its social policy, at a time when the reports of the Royal Commission on the Poor Law had quickened interest in welfare issues. Both the terms of the contest and their own financial and organisational problems prevented Labour from mounting an independent challenge to Liberalism. As Martin Pugh has observed, Labour's successes in 1910 were obtained within the framework of the revived electoral pact with the Liberals. Where Labour and Liberal candidates came into conflict, it was almost always the Liberal who did the better of the two.[23] The occurrence of two general elections in rapid succession imposed a severe strain on the Labour machine. Thus in January 1910 the party ran 78 candidates, received a total of 505,657 votes and returned 40 MPs. In December it secured 42 seats, but it fielded only 56 candidates and its vote fell accordingly to 371,802 (6.4 per cent as against 7.0 per cent in January).[24] The apparent increase in the number of Labour victories over 1906 was accounted for by the affiliation of the Miners' Federation MPs to the Labour party rather than by any genuine access of support.[25] Labour seats won at by-elections in the 1906 Parliament like Jarrow and Colne Valley were regained by the Liberals. Of the 35 three-way contests that took place in 1910, Labour won none, was second in only six and came third in the remaining twenty-nine.[26]

On the face of it, there was no significant improvement in Labour's fortunes in the remaining years before the First World War. The party made no further gains at by-elections and lost all four of the seats which it had to defend.[27] One of these, admittedly, was the special case of Bow and Bromley, where George Lansbury resigned his seat to fight a by-election on the sole question of women's suffrage. But the others were mining constituencies where the Liberals showed every sign of being able to sustain a Lib-Lab electoral tradition. Labour's most spectacular defeat came at Hanley in July 1912, its candidate being beaten into third place by the radical land reformer, R. L. Outhwaite. Indeed Labour candidates regularly came bottom of the poll in contests in industrial seats. The argument that this was due to the 'franchise factor' which artificially disenfranchised potential Labour voters has now been largely exploded, since Duncan Tanner has shown that at least as many middle class as working class voters were denied the vote by the operation of the registration system. In any case, it is clear from the by-election results that many trade unionists preferred to vote for Liberal (or even Conservative) rather than Labour candidates. Certainly there are few signs that the Labour party was making an irresistible electoral advance.[28]

Even so, a measure of balance is necessary in interpreting the available evidence. The circumstances of the 1910 elections may have been uniquely unfavourable to Labour. The impact of the Osborne judgement on the party's finances was serious. Despite its lack of by-election success, on other fronts the Labour party was strengthening its position before 1914. There was a modest, if patchy, improvement in its performance at municipal elections. In 1907, successful Labour candidates numbered 86; in 1913 the figure rose to 196.[29] Party membership was growing. Trade union affiliations rose from 975,000 in 1906 to 1,858,000 in 1912, those of the socialist societies from 17,000 to 33,000. By 1913 there were 143 affiliated local bodies (Trades Councils or local Labour parties) compared with 73 in 1906. Ballots held under the terms of the 1913 Trade Union Act showed substantial majorities in favour of establishing trade union political funds for Labour's support. The party had launched its own newspaper, the *Daily Citizen* (in addition to Lansbury's more exciting *Daily Herald*). It was building up its staff of full-time organisers and party agents and by 1914 could contemplate running over a hundred candidates at the next general election. Rank-and-file dissatisfaction with the constraints imposed on the constituencies by the electoral pact with the Liberals (which was already breaking down at by-elections) put pressure on party leaders to abandon the progressive alliance strategy.[30]

Similarly, although there was sustained criticism of the parliamentary party's lacklustre performance (voiced in publications such as *Is the Parliamentary Party a Failure?* in 1908 and the ILP's *Let Us Reform the Labour Party* in 1910), under Ramsay MacDonald's chairmanship from 1911–14 the Labour party began to carve out a record of greater political achievement. This owed something to the changed parliamentary position as a result of the 1910 elections. The Liberals had lost their overall majority and were dependent on Irish and Labour support. But it should be noted that Labour did not have the capacity to defeat the government on its own, even if it voted with the Conservatives. The party's reluctance to face another early election limited the leverage which could be exerted on the Liberal government. In these circumstances MacDonald played his hand with some skill. He secured the enactment of payment of MPs in return for promising Labour support for the government's programme of constitutional reform and national insurance. In 1913 he won the even more important concession of the Trade Union Act, which undid the effects of the Osborne judgement by allowing the trade unions to create political funds, provided the leaders were authorised to do so by a ballot of their members. MacDonald was personally so successful in his dealings with Liberal ministers that there was even some discussion of his taking office in a Liberal-Labour coalition government.

Yet while these developments might suggest a strengthening of the progressive alliance and possibly even the merging of the Liberal and Labour parties into a combined progressive party, the reality was rather different. There were still Lib-Lab trade unionists in the Labour ranks, but the Labour party as an organisation was possessed of a centrifugal momentum that was taking it further away from the Liberal party and creating a subordinate but distinctive place for it within the Edwardian political system. The debate over the Liberal government's social legislation, to which reference has already been made, showed that Labour was capable of expounding coherent differences between its own policies and those of the Liberals, for instance over the question of whether the reforms should be funded wholly from taxation or from workers' contributions. Labour did not benefit electorally from the initial unpopularity of the Liberal insurance schemes, but neither did the New Liberalism seem likely to guarantee the Liberal party's political future. Working class suspicions of the capitalist state gave the Labour party a long-term base of appeal against the two major parties. Even more was this the case in the industrial arena. The discontent of 1910–12 had forced some concessions from the Liberal government, but the Liberals were still seen as too much of a middle class, employers' party. In areas like South Wales the use of troops and the identification of the Liberals with the employers' interests had hardened a sense of trade union solidarity which Labour rather than the Liberals was better placed to exploit.[31] If MacDonald's Labour party could not do so, there were others – such as the syndicalists, or the members of the British Socialist Party (formed in 1911 by members of the old SDF and Graysonite ILP-ers) – who were prepared to take up the challenge.

In short, the Liberals had found no more than a temporary answer to the electoral dimension of the Labour question prior to 1914. Whatever its weaknesses, the appearance of an independent Labour party in parliament after 1906 was a major change in the party political system. With its solid base of trade union support it represented a partial institutionalisation of industrial conflict in the political sphere of the kind which Liberal politicians in particular had always striven to prevent. That the industrial unrest of the pre-war period did not lead to an immediate upsurge in Labour support may suggest that the Labour threat was containable; certainly there was no realistic prospect of the return of a Labour government. Yet in a sense the warnings of Lloyd George and other Liberals were being borne out. Labour was siphoning off a certain amount of Liberal support. Its existence, and its survival in difficult conditions, provided at least a potential alternative to the duopoly of the two 'capitalist' parties. The New Liberalism, which had developed as a response to Labour's rise, could not wholly restore the status quo ante-1906. Partly this was because the New Liberals themselves were unable to become the dominant group in the Liberal party, not even in the cabinet, let alone in the constituencies.[32] But there was a more fundamental reason as well, namely that the New Liberalism, with its emphasis on state-sponsored social reforms and a state-regulated compromise between capital and labour, did not play the tunes that an embattled Labour movement wanted to hear. It was carefully calculated to reconcile the divergent strands of Liberal opinion, but to a sectional trade union movement, concerned primarily with the defence of its own interests, a separate Labour party seemed a better guarantee of a fair deal from the institutions of a political system still controlled largely by the wealthy middle classes.

The Labour Question and the Coming of War

It is a commonplace of historical analysis to argue that the outbreak of war in August 1914 was the prelude to vast and unexpected changes in the British political and industrial system. So it was.[33] The war shattered the Liberal party, led to a massive, if in most cases temporary, extension of state control over industry and provided the trade unions and the Labour party with an opportunity to increase their status and influence in national life. At the same time, according to the views of George Dangerfield, writing in the 1930s, the Great War, far from precipitating a revolution, may actually have prevented one. In his beguiling classic, *The Strange Death of Liberal England*, first published in 1935, he suggested that events were moving towards a crisis before the assassinations at Sarajevo. The three interrelated challenges of syndicalist-inspired labour unrest, Irish nationalism and the women's suffrage campaign were symptoms of a deep polarisation of political attitudes and of a predisposition to reject parliamentarism and the rule of law which together threatened fatally to undermine the fabric of British society as the Edwardians and the Victorians before them had known it. By implication, the First World War, though unquestionably cataclysmic, was almost a lesser evil than the incipient anarchy which was stalking the country in the summer of 1914.

Insofar as the Labour question was concerned, Dangerfield's thesis was somewhat overdrawn. Arguably the peak of the pre-war unrest had passed by 1914. The Triple Alliance had made no plans for co-ordinated action. The influence of the syndicalists was strong among the rank-and-file in areas like South Wales but they did not represent the views of a majority of the Labour movement. There was no obvious linkage between the labour troubles and the struggles of the Irish or the suffragettes, although there were some individual points of contact. For all the appearances of conflict, the history of the Edwardian period reflected the sturdily non-revolutionary character of most labour agitation. The Labour party was content to operate within the confines of the parliamentary system, even though that system was, for the moment, biased against it. On the industrial side, most Labour leaders still sought to achieve their aims by negotiation, with strike action as a last resort. The use of conciliation machinery was spreading, even in industries most affected by disruption. Trade union leaders were willing to co-operate with employers and government on both an official and unofficial basis, meeting ministers for high level discussions or participating in enquiries and committees set up by government departments. Beneath the surface turmoil, a more clearly defined triangular relationship was developing, with employers, government and unions each playing their part. Of course suspicions and hostilities remained, underlain by real class tensions, but the evolutionary tendencies of the system were undeniable.

In another way, however, the sense of an impending clash was nearer the mark. The Edwardian period had seen a growing involvement of government in many aspects of industrial life. Under Liberal guidance this interventionism had two main purposes. One was to ensure that, as Campbell-Bannerman put it in 1906, 'the two rival powers of capital and labour' were placed 'on an equality so that the fight between them, so far as fight is necessary, should be at least a fair one. . . . ' [34] The other was to see that the fight between the rival powers did not harm the interests of the community at large. The Liberals had made a number of concessions to Labour since 1905, the Trades Disputes Act being perhaps the most important. But there were bound to be times when concession had to be balanced by restraint, or when the policies of government and Labour diverged. By intervening in industrial disputes the government placed itself in a position potentially antagonistic to the unions if it was unable fully to endorse their demands. Even the introduction of the Liberal social reforms brought the government and Labour into conflict, since the unions saw themselves as upholding their voluntarist, self-help principles (ironically those of the old Liberalism, if not of the new) against an encroaching, welfarist state. Such a divergence of views was not the stuff from which revolutions were made, but it did make the accommodation of Labour within a new social dispensation more difficult. There remained the further possibility that rising levels of industrial unrest would force the government to reopen the question of legal limitations on trade union power, as the employers and some Conservative politicians were already demanding.[35]

The coming of war seemed to make conflict between organised Labour and the state more rather than less likely.[36] Although in the early months of the war the government followed a 'business as usual' approach which maintained the existing private enterprise system, the Defence of the Realm Act of 1914 gave ministers sweeping if vaguely defined special powers which could be used to clamp down on industrial unrest, curtail the activities of opposition groups and mobilise manpower and resources for the war effort. The prospect of a confrontation was increased because it could not be assumed that the Labour movement would automatically support the war. Labour leaders had been active in the international socialist movement before 1914 and there had been some discussion of using the power of the workers in belligerent countries to halt an 'imperialist' war. Prominent figures, like Keir Hardie and Ramsay MacDonald, the chairman of Labour's parliamentary party, were outright opponents of the decision to go to war. On 5 August, the day after war was declared, a special conference of Labour, Co-operative, trade union and socialist groups, while not opposing the war, voted to establish a War Emergency Workers' National Committee to ensure that wartime conditions did not lead to the unacceptable erosion of working class standards of living.

Yet in fact, in its early stages, the war appealed overwhelmingly to the collaborationist rather than the confrontational instincts of the Labour movement. MacDonald found himself in a minority in the parliamentary party and resigned the chairmanship in favour of Arthur Henderson. The Labour party officially supported the government's declaration of war and agreed to a wartime political truce in which the parties undertook not to oppose each other's candidates at by-elections. On 2 September the TUC Parliamentary Committee, most of its members imbued with patriotic feeling, agreed to support a national recruiting campaign. The Labour leadership attempted to match the political truce with an industrial one. On 24 August a meeting of Labour's Joint Board (including representatives of the Labour party, the TUC Parliamentary Committee and the General Federation of Trade Unions) adopted a resolution calling for 'an immediate effort ... to terminate all existing trade disputes' and to prevent the occurrence of future strikes or lock-outs.[37]

The Joint Board's appeal had an immediate effect in reducing the number of disputes, but in the conditions which prevailed in the winter of 1914–15 it was difficult to prevent rank-and-file grievances from breaking out in unofficial actions. Inflationary pressures generated demands for higher wages as prices soared. While the demands of war production stimulated some industries others were left in depression. Shortages of skilled labour led to pressure on the unions to agree to the lifting of some established trade practices and the 'dilution' of skilled labour with semi-skilled or unskilled workers, including women. Another cause of labour dissatisfaction was the belief (accurate enough in some cases) that businesses employed in war production were making large profits that were not being passed on to the workers. The engineering industry, which was pivotal to the whole war effort, was particularly badly affected by these problems. The Clydeside engineers' strike of February 1915, organised by the shop stewards' Central Withdrawal of Labour Committee, an unofficial body, was symptomatic of the sense of grievance at what was felt to be the unevenness of sacrifice which the war was demanding.

The problems of the shipbuilding and engineering trades, which disrupted munitions production, and continuing unrest in the mines, made it apparent that high level government action was needed. Before the end of 1914 Sir George Askwith had been appointed to head the Treasury Committee on Production to find ways of improving the supply of manpower to industry and increasing output. In March 1915, as a consequence of the Clyde strike and other disputes, representatives of the unions were invited to the Treasury to discuss the problems of wartime labour with Lloyd George. The result was the 'Treasury Agreement', by which the unions agreed to temporary relaxation of trade practices for the duration of the war and to the compulsory arbitration of wartime trade disputes, in return for a promise that a tax would be imposed on excess war profits and that local 'production committees' would be established on which the unions would be represented.[38] Lloyd George described the agreement as 'a charter for Labour'. Its real significance, though, was that it enlisted Labour support for government direction of the war effort, reducing the threat of confrontation between Labour and the state. Although, as will be seen, the working of the Treasury Agreement was not without friction, and some trade unionists felt cheated by the government's failure to fulfil all of its promises, the fact remained that the government and the unions had entered into partnership for a common purpose in a way that had not been possible before 1914.

Labour's integration into the industrial side of the war effort was followed by its closer involvement in the political direction of the war as well. When Asquith formed his coalition government in May 1915 Arthur Henderson accepted the invitation to join the cabinet as President of the Board of Education and, in effect, the government's chief adviser on labour problems. Whether as the last purely Liberal ministry capitulated to its opponents under the pressures of total war it had belatedly found the answer to the Labour question which had eluded it earlier in its existence remained to be seen.

3
THE LABOUR QUESTION IN WAR AND PEACE, 1915–26

The Treasury Agreement and the inclusion of Labour in the first wartime coalition were attempts to harness Labour support for the war effort and to delegate to the Labour leadership responsibility for the management of labour problems for the duration of the war. In return, Labour was to be given some influence over policy, through Henderson's membership of the cabinet and trade union representation on the plethora of committees which the industrial conduct of the war required. Yet the integration of Labour into the framework of government was never complete. Labour leaders were not admitted to an equal share in the direction of policy, nor were they successful in controlling their own rank-and-file and preventing industrial unrest. In 1918 Labour's uneasy accommodation with the state broke down. The Labour party left the coalition and decided to fight for power on its own account. The end of the political truce was accompanied by the termination of the industrial truce, or what was left of it – a process hastened by the rush with which Lloyd George's government dismantled the system of wartime controls. The levels of discontent in 1919–21 matched, and even exceeded, those of the Edwardian period. The political interlude of the first Labour government in 1924 did little to halt the alienation of workers from the state, merely emphasising the differences between the political and trade union wings of the Labour movement. The process of alienation seemed to reach its logical conclusion in the open confrontation between government and unions in the 'General Strike' of 1926.

War and Coalition, 1915–18

The First World War was above all else an industrial war. That is to say, its outcome depended on the industrial capacity of the belligerent states and their ability to mobilise that capacity for military purposes. Manpower, too, was a crucial element in the quest for victory, both for the armed forces and for the maintenance of industrial and agricultural production. At first the Liberal government in power in Britain in 1914 took only limited steps towards organising the country's industrial and manpower resources more effectively. The war was expected to be a short one. The main emphasis in the early weeks was on financial measures to ensure that the demands of increased expenditure could be met. Recruitment for the armed forces remained on a voluntary basis until the introduction of conscription in 1916. But by the winter of 1914–15 it was clear that more stringent changes in the 'business-as-usual' regime were necessary. The unchecked enlistment of skilled engineering workers for military service had caused serious problems of labour supply in the munitions industry.[1] Askwith's Committee on Production revealed other shortcomings and deficiencies. The scandal of the 'shells shortage' which arose in the spring of 1915 and helped to trigger the formation of the coalition government finally tipped the scales in favour of a more interventionist, 'efficiency-led' approach. A new Ministry of Munitions was created, with Lloyd George at its head.[2] The practice of co-opting businessmen like Eric Geddes and Lord Rhondda into government service to clear bottlenecks in production and expedite the delivery of supplies was stepped up. By the end of 1916 the government had taken direct control (though not ownership) of whole swathes of

British industry, including shipping, the railways and the mines.

The recruitment of leading industrialists to man the war machine, together with the enlarged role of the state in the organisation of industrial life, imparted a much more managerial appearance to the wartime coalitions, especially after 1916, than had been exhibited even by the interventionist Liberal administrations of the pre-war period. Within the new structure labour questions were important mainly insofar as they affected productivity and performance, rather than for straightforwardly political reasons. The regulation of labour and the control of the labour market came to be seen as an imperative of victory. In this respect the Treasury Agreement, welcome as it was in offering an earnest of union co-operation and goodwill, did not provide a complete answer to the government's problems. It was a purely voluntary undertaking, with no legal force. Its value was reduced by the refusal of the Miners' Federation to adhere to it and by the reservations of the engineers, whose leaders were won over only by the promise of more concessions. In June 1915, therefore, the new coalition government sought to give the provisions of the agreement statutory effect by introducing the Munitions of War Act. This gave ministers the power to designate all factories or enterprises involved in war production as 'controlled establishments' in which strikes and lock-outs were declared illegal and all disputes were to be settled by the compulsory arbitration of 'munitions tribunals'. The Act imposed a limit on profits of 20 per cent above 1914 levels, which was welcomed by the unions without being punitive to the owners. Less popular with the workers were the provisions for the dilution of skilled labour and for the introduction of 'leaving certificates' which had to be obtained from their employers by all workers wishing to leave jobs in the munitions industry, even to transfer from one firm to another.

In dealing with unions of skilled workers, whose bargaining position had been greatly strengthened by the coming of war, appeasement was often a more practical recourse than compulsion, however. The limitations of the Munitions of War Act were swiftly revealed by a dispute in the South Wales coalfields in July 1915. The miners rejected as inadequate a pay award and 200,000 of them went on strike in defiance of a proclamation ruling such action illegal under the new legislation. Only Lloyd George's rapid departure for South Wales by special train and the immediate improvement of the pay offer got the men back to work. Elsewhere even Lloyd George's silver-tongued exhortations fell on deaf ears, as when he and Henderson were roughly greeted by angry munitions workers during a tour of Clydeside in December 1915.[3] Rank-and-file discontent, orchestrated by the shop stewards movement, gathered pace as wartime inflation continued to erode incomes. Various concessions were made – the introduction of rent and price controls, minimum wage provisions for selected workers, a Trade Card scheme to be administered by the engineering unions giving their members exemption from military conscription – but still the embers of unrest fanned periodically into flame. Yet despite the occasional application of a repressive hand (as in the arrest and deportation of the Clydeside shop stewards in 1916) the government stopped short of imposing full industrial conscription, realising the difficulties involved in any such plan and preferring instead to rely on the quasi-voluntary arrangements made with the trade unions, with the threat of more draconian laws as an inducement to co-operation.

Lloyd George, first as Minister of Munitions and then as Prime Minister, made every effort to conciliate Labour opinion. When he formed his coalition government in December 1916 he met members of the Labour party's national executive personally to argue the case for Labour participation in the new administration. On Labour ministers agreeing to serve, Henderson became a member of the five-man War Cabinet and two other Labour men – John Hodge and George Barnes – got cabinet posts. Barnes was made Minister of Pensions, Hodge became the first head of the newly-created Ministry of Labour. This last innovation was itself recognition of the wartime importance of labour questions, even if the overlapping jurisdictions of the several departments responsible for dealing with them did not always make for clarity of policy.[4] Practical measures were introduced to meet specific grievances. Lloyd George also tried to rally Labour opinion in other ways. He responded to the growing demand for a 'democratic peace' by outlining his war aims to an audience of trade unionists in January 1918.[5] There was an attempt, too, to catch the tide of feeling in favour of using the enhanced powers which the state had acquired in wartime for peaceful purposes. In 1917 Lloyd George appointed his close colleague Christopher Addison as Minister of Reconstruction. Although the activities of the new ministry have been dismissed as no more than 'windowdressing, to allay labour discontent'[6] their positive aspects should not be underrated. Notable schemes of housing, health and educational reform were planned.[7] There was also a search for a more co-operative framework for post-war industrial relations. The Whitley Committee on the relations of Employers and Employed, which had been meeting since 1916, recommended the setting up of an integrated system of works, district and national councils for each industry, to place negotiations on a more stable and harmonious footing.[8] An Industrial Court was to be created, to arbitrate in otherwise intractable disputes.

The experience of war had thus obviously acted to force the pace of government thinking on the welfare and industrial relations aspects of the Labour question, as on wider questions of social reform and manpower planning. But this did not necessarily lead to a closer relationship between organised Labour and the state. Partly this was because the proposed reforms, however attractive they might seem (and this itself was a matter for doubt, as the Liberals had found before 1914), had little appeal in the short term context of rising prices, food shortages and growing war weariness evident by the latter part of 1917. Industrial unrest rose sharply in the last two years of the war. A strike of 200,000 engineering workers in London, the Midlands and the North of England in April and May 1917 was symptomatic. In 1917 as a whole there were 730 stoppages and a total of 5.6 million working days were lost through industrial action (compared with 532 stoppages and 2.4 million days in 1916). In 1918 the figures were 1,165 stoppages and 5.8 million days lost.[9] These were admittedly below the immediate pre-war levels, but given the patriotic pressures of wartime (not to mention the legal constraints of the Munitions of War Act) they betokened a more general disaffection.

Labour's rank-and-file ambivalence, even hostility, towards the government had a second, deeper cause. Notwithstanding the Labour party's membership of the coalition, and the involvement of union leaders in production committees and a variety of other administrative functions, in many ways the war seemed to have established a closer congruence between the government and the employers. This was true on a personal level. For example, William Weir, the Director of Munitions for Scotland, responsible for dealing with the unrest on Clydeside, was one of the largest employers of labour in the industry. The employers co-opted into the government structure generally appeared to exercise a much greater degree of influence than their trade union counterparts, particularly once the Conservative party had increased its share of coalition patronage in 1916 to augment Lloyd George's personal preference for self-made men. As a body, the industrialists made their presence felt by forming the Federation of British Industries in 1916, as a counterweight to the TUC. Even if the government did not in this way exactly come under the sway of the employers, the war had in any case made the state, at least at one remove, more of an employer in its own right, sharpening the potential for conflict between it and the workers. The government's sensitivity to the interests of private capital seemed in marked contrast to its willingness to coerce labour, and the idea of inequality of sacrifice was a potent source of grievance. The euphoria with which the Russian Revolution of 1917 was greeted added a further ingredient to the cocktail of discontent, strengthening calls for the introduction of genuine public ownership of industry in place of the government-administered capitalism offered by the coalition. In June 1917, at a conference of trade unionists, ILP-ers and members of the BSP in Leeds, resolutions were passed calling for the establishment in Britain of workers' and soldiers' councils on the Russian model.

Changing attitudes to the war and the government's increasing unpopularity with sections of the Labour movement naturally had their effect on the politics of the Labour party. Throughout the war the party's leaders had a difficult path to tread. The outbreak of war had produced a split between the ILP minority and the rest of the parliamentary party. MacDonald, one of the party's few figures of national stature, felt bound to resign the chairmanship of Labour's parliamentary group because of his reluctance to vote for war credits. Keir Hardie died in 1915, his last days saddened by the clamour of a war of which he could not approve. Although initially most trade union and moderate Labour opinion supported the war, even the party's decision to participate in the wartime coalitions was potentially disruptive. It enhanced Labour's standing as a partner in government and gave leaders like Henderson some experience of office, but it brought no other political gains, serving merely to heighten the pre-war tensions between the party leaders and the rank-and-file of the Labour movement. The trade unions, and other organisations such as the War Emergency Workers' National Committee, bore the brunt of the task of defending the workers' economic interests while Labour ministers seemed to be adopting an almost exclusively governmental perspective. There was criticism of the fact that Labour was able to win few real concessions for its co-operation in the war effort. Conscription was opposed both by the Labour party and the TUC, even though Labour ministers shared collective responsibility for its introduction. With their critics accusing them of having sold out to Lloyd George, the Labour leaders saw industrial unrest threatening to undermine their authority within the party and push the Labour movement towards more extreme forms of 'Direct Action'.

In the last eighteen months of the war, however, an important change occurred. The Labour party succeeded in regaining a measure of cohesion and distancing itself from the Lloyd George government, even though technically remaining a member of the coalition until the armistice. There were two unifying factors at work. One was the question of war aims. By 1917 all sections of the Labour movement, irrespective of their original attitudes to the war, were in favour of a 'democratic' peace and the creation of a League of Nations as a central feature of the post-war settlement. The Russian Revolution of February 1917 had encouraged thoughts of a negotiated end to the war as the best way of saving the infant Russian republic from defeat at the hands of Germany. Indeed, Henderson had visited Russia in June 1917 and returned to Britain with a proposal to send delegates to an international socialist conference in Stockholm at which the idea of a compromise peace with Germany was to be explored. The proposal was warmly supported by the Labour party but Henderson was refused permission by the War Cabinet to attend any congress at which German delegates were to be present. It was this issue, forever associated in popular mythology with the humiliation of the 'doormat incident' (when Henderson was kept waiting outside the cabinet room in which his position was discussed by his colleagues),[10] which prompted Henderson's personal resignation from the government, his place in the War Cabinet being taken by George Barnes.

Henderson's resignation constituted a turning point in war-time Labour politics and was, indirectly, the second unifying factor at work in 1917–18. Freed from the constraints of office, Henderson, in his capacity as secretary of the party, was able to devote himself wholeheartedly to the task of preparing Labour for the electoral battles ahead. The split in the Liberal party which followed Asquith's refusal to join the Lloyd George government, and the way in which the war had dramatised the conflict between an essentially 'capitalist' coalition and the organised working class gave the Labour party an unprecedented opportunity to make an impact on post-war politics, if only it could seize it. To this end, a new party programme, *Labour and the New Social Order* (drafted by Sidney Webb) and a new constitution (which permitted individual membership of local Labour parties and included Clause Four, committing the party to achieving the 'common ownership of the means of production')[11] were adopted, giving Labour a distinctively socialist identity it had not possessed before 1914 and creating an organisational framework for further expansion.

The number of affiliated constituency bodies was increased from 199 in 1916 to 389 in 1918; trade union affiliated membership had risen to 2.9 million by the same date. Confident of their growing strength, and aware of the mood of their supporters, Labour leaders ruled out any continuation of the coalition beyond the end of the war. Henderson contemplated running 500 candidates when the election came, transforming Labour from its pre-war status as a parliamentary pressure group into a fully independent party capable of challenging for power.[12] The war which in 1915 seemed to have brought organised Labour and the state into a more harmonious relationship, politically and industrially, had thus by 1918 driven them further apart, stiffening Labour's determination to gain control of the state for purposes of its own.

Lloyd George and Labour, 1918–22

The end of the war brought the end of the wartime coalition. Lloyd George retained the support of a small group of Labour MPs, led by George Barnes, but the official Labour party moved into opposition. At the election of December 1918, though, Lloyd George was confirmed in power, despite the best efforts of Labour and the non-Lloyd George Liberals. His refashioned coalition of Conservatives, Liberals and 'national' Labour won a landslide victory. The Prime Minister embarked upon the process of peacemaking at Versailles and of building a land 'fit for heroes' at home. Yet apotheosis was followed by nemesis. Within four years the coalition had broken up and Lloyd George's long ministerial career was over. His downfall was the result of the conjunction of a number of factors, personal and political. Nothing so signally demonstrated the failure of the coalition, however, as the failure of its economic and industrial policies. This is not to say that the Labour question caused the collapse of the Lloyd George government, but it certainly played its part.[13]

These were heady times for the Labour movement. The pre-war expansion of the trade unions had continued throughout the war and was sustained into the immediate post-war period. In 1918 trade union membership stood at 6.5 million; by 1920 it had risen to 8.3 million. For all the signs of discontent, the war had brought many benefits to union members. It had created a higher-wage, full-employment economy. These conditions were perpetuated by the post-war boom. Trade union organisation had strengthened its grip on previously unorganised sections of the working population. Between 1914 and 1920, for example, the proportion of women workers who were members of trade unions rose from 9 to 24 per cent.[14] Although it is a contentious claim among historians, it seems likely that there had been an increase in solidarity and class consciousness among ordinary workers as the labour force had become more homogenised.[15] Certainly expectations had been raised by the experience of wartime collectivism (limited in some respects though it was), by talk of 'Reconstruction' and by the growing feeling that 'socialism' (however ill-defined) had become a practical proposition. The gospel of 'Direct Action' inherited from the pre-war syndicalists was appealing to the trade union rank-and-file. Even the official leaders of the unions were organising themselves with more ambition and a greater sense of purpose than before 1914. The TUC replaced its primarily lobbyist Parliamentary Committee with a General Council (as some saw it, 'general staff') in 1921. The drive for amalgamation made possible by the 1917 Amalgamations Act produced a formidable phalanx of powerful unions: the Amalgamated Engineering Union in 1921, the Transport and General Workers (1923), the General and Municipal Workers in 1924. The pre-war Triple Alliance of miners, railwaymen and transport workers was revived in 1919.[16]

Lloyd George's government consequently faced widespread labour unrest in 1918–19. In the minds of ministers fearful of the spread of 'Bolshevism' and influenced by the spectre of revolution in Ireland and upheaval in Europe there was the possibility too that the wave of strikes could turn into something altogether more apocalyptic than the ordinary run of industrial disputes. These feelings were heightened by the occurrence of police strikes and mutinies in the army occasioned by the slow pace of demobilisation. Most of the trouble, however, fell into a more familiar, if no less worrying, pattern. In January 1919 the Clydeside engineers once again went on strike, this time to demand a 40 hour week. Simultaneously, the Miners' Federation balloted its members in favour of a strike to secure nationalisation of the mines, together with a 30 per cent wage increase and a six hour working day. In September there was a national rail strike following what the unions regarded as an inadequate pay offer. In the last two cases, of course, the government was a direct party to the disputes because the railways and mines were still under wartime state control. Indeed, one effect of the wartime policy had been to place the government more and more in the front line of industrial conflict, reducing its capacity to play the honest broker as it had attempted to do in similar circumstances before 1914.

Responses, though, still followed mainly pre-war lines (perhaps inevitably, since the government had given up its compulsory arbitration powers under the Munitions of War Act at the close of hostilities). Coercion was used in a more thoroughgoing way in some instances. The Clydeside engineers were cowed into submission by the despatch of troops and tanks to the streets of Glasgow, reflecting the government's alarm at the prospects of the shop stewards movement there emulating the deeds of the Petrograd soviet. A Cabinet Committee on Industrial Unrest received reports from Special Branch agents and Home Office sources in an atmosphere somewhat reminiscent of the days of Pitt, Liverpool and Oliver the Spy.[17] In 1920 an Emergency Powers Act was passed to ensure that essential services could be maintained in the event of a general stoppage of work. But ministers avoided confrontation with the unions whenever possible. In the case of the mines and the railways, conscious of its responsibilities to the community and its role as a surrogate employer, the government made concessions and played for time. The miners were persuaded to call off their strike by the appointment of the Sankey Commission to enquire into the coal industry and make recommendations about its future. The railwaymen received an improved pay offer which got them back to work. By 1919–20 the first fruits of Reconstruction were beginning to filter through with the introduction of the 1918 Education Act and the extension of unemployment insurance and minimum wage schemes, although there is no evidence to suggest that these had any impact on the levels of labour unrest.[18]

As in the pre-war period, *ad hoc* concessions and a more dispersed policy of welfarism were complemented by attempts to establish permanent structures for conciliation and co-operation. Lloyd George addressed a meeting of eight hundred employers and trade unionists in February 1919, the outcome of which was the formation of the National Industrial Conference, a body which was to meet twice-yearly to discuss the problems of industry and to consider reports from committees and working parties convened to investigate particular issues. To supplement the 'grand durbar' approach of the NIC, the Ministry of Labour pressed ahead with the introduction of Whitley Councils (of which 41 had been established by July 1919) and with the plan for an Industrial Court to which employers and unions could present their cases for arbitration. The efficacy of these reforms, and even the degree of sincerity behind them, has nevertheless been questioned, and with good reason. The NIC was almost a complete failure, even as a safety valve, and had little impact on industrial relations, which, as before, were conducted either between unions and individual employers or under the auspices of national conciliation boards. It did little to improve the climate of relations between employers and unions and had no influence on government economic or industrial policy. Similarly the Whitley Councils took a firm hold in few places in the private sector, fulfilling a real function only in public service departments. The major industries preferred to rely on their existing machinery (or lack of it) and a number of those Councils which were set up in the first flush of enthusiasm later fell into disuse. The Industrial Court likewise failed to become a permanent feature of the industrial relations scene, although its potential usefulness was demonstrated by the judgement in favour of the dock workers' case for a national minimum wage as a result of the Shaw Inquiry of 1920, during which the unions were ably represented by the architect of the Transport and General Workers' amalgamation, the 'dockers' KC', Ernest Bevin.[19]

While some disputes were settled by peaceful means, elsewhere the level of unrest continued to rise. In 1919 there were 1352 stoppages, costing 34.9 million working days. The number of days lost fell slightly, to 26.5 million, in 1920 (though the total of stoppages rose to 1607), but in 1921 it reached the unprecedented figure of 85.8 million (more than twice that for 1912, the worst year of the pre-war period).[20] The unions showed their willingness to use industrial muscle for political as well as economic purposes. In 1920 Councils of Action were formed to support the dockers who refused to load the *Jolly George*, a cargo ship carrying arms to aid the Poles in their war against Soviet Russia. It is true that too much should not be made of this particular episode. The unions' stand probably did not influence government policy and it had no direct sequel. More generally, the government's firm action against the Clydeside engineers had broken the strength of the shop stewards movement and reduced the influence of quasi-syndicalist groups who wanted to use industrial action for political ends. The Communist Party of Great Britain, founded in 1921, fought an uphill battle to reverse the engrained 'economism' of the trade union leadership, without any apparent success. By 1921–2 there were signs that the number of disputes was falling anyway, as the post-war boom came to an end and depression began to bite. By the middle of 1921 over two million people were unemployed, accounting for some 17.8 per cent of the insured population, as opposed to the 2.4 per cent out of work in 1919.[21]

Yet in some ways the impact of depression made those disputes that did take place all the more bitter. In 1919–20, with the economy booming and the labour market buoyant, employers could afford to concede wage rises. By 1921, as Britain's export industries felt the full effect of collapsing markets, the unions had been forced into a long rearguard action to maintain wage levels, preserve jobs and protect living standards. They fought these battles at a time when their own membership was being depleted by rising unemployment. From a total of 8.3 million in 1920, trade union membership slumped to 6.6 million in 1921 and 5.4 million in 1923. The negotiating stance of the employers hardened and the government, implementing its own plans of deflationary cuts in public spending, had little to offer by way of relief.

Once again it was the coal industry that was at the heart of post-war industrial strife. The experience of the miners encapsulated the raised hopes and eventual frustrations of many within the Labour movement at this time. The course of the conflict in the coal industry also exercised an important influence on the history of the Labour movement and the shape of the Labour question in the 1920s and beyond. The miners, numbering one and a quarter million in 1920 and heavily unionised, were the shock troops of the industrial workforce. Time and again they had used their strategic position to wring concessions from a reluctant government, both before and during the war. After the war they sought final victory over the coalowners by securing outright nationalisation of the mines, threatening strike action in support of the demand at the beginning of 1919. The Sankey Commission – the appointment of which, as has been seen, postponed the threatened strike – went some way towards accepting the union's case, Sankey's report opting tentatively for a reorganisation of the industry under state control. The opposition of the owners and of the Conservative majority in the coalition government made nationalisation impossible, however. Lloyd George finally admitted as much in August. The Labour party and the TUC joined the Miners' Federation in a 'Mines for the Nation' campaign, but no progress was made.

The collapse of the export market for coal and the drop in coal prices shifted the focus from nationalisation to wages. In October 1920 the miners went on strike in support of a claim for a wage increase. Faced with the threat of sympathetic action by the railwaymen and the transport workers under the revived Triple Alliance, the government offered a six-month increase and promised to discuss with the owners the setting up of a national wages board. However, they also announced the impending decontrol of the industry and its return to private management. Initially set for 31 August 1921, the decontrol date was subsequently advanced to 31 March, without any steps being taken towards the creation of the national board. The owners instead sought wage reductions and a return to district bargaining. When the miners resisted, a lock-out was imposed, beginning on 1 April.

The attempt of the Miners' Federation to repeat the successful tactic of the previous October ended in failure. Arrangements were made with the other members of the Triple Alliance for an embargo on the movement of coal to begin on 16 April. But, on what became known in trade union annals as 'Black Friday', 15 April, the miners' partners called off the threatened action, largely because of apparent indecision on the part of the miners' leaders about the future course of the dispute.[22] The solidarity of their alliance broken, the miners were eventually forced to capitulate and to accept a reduction in wages before returning to work on the owners' terms. The effects of Black Friday were far-reaching for the trade union movement, even if the defeat of 1921 was not the end of the miners' struggle, as the events of 1926 – and in some senses of the 1970s and 1980s – were to prove.

What verdict, then, should be passed on the handling of labour problems by the Lloyd George government? On a purely negative level it can be said that the coalition rode out the storm much as Asquith's government had before the war, using a variety of expedients to divide the unions and to prevent the development of any broad-based revolutionary threat (supposing this ever to have been a possibility). Such a strategy would have been in line with the essentially Conservative, anti-Labour character of much of the government's support. Equally, some writers would argue that there was a more positive, if basically social-imperialist, aspect to the coalition's labour policy, raising its claims to be considered as a government of 'National Efficiency' or alternatively to represent a revival of pre-war New Liberalism in a different guise.[23] It is true that, during the war at least, there were attempts to create a 'higher unity', by involving Labour in the machinery of government and in the industrial administration of the war. Industries were taken into government control and a much more rigorous organisation of the labour market, wages and prices was imposed. There is evidence that Lloyd George hoped to perpetuate some of these innovations into the peace, as witnessed by the Reconstruction plans and the efforts to create a more formal, semi-corporatist structure for industrial relations which would foster greater harmony of interest between capital and labour. Yet ultimately all this came to nothing. The new system of industrial relations was no different in substance from the old. The wartime controls were swiftly dismantled after 1918 and private ownership was allowed to flourish – or not to flourish – without restraint. In the process, Labour was alienated from the institutions of government more completely than before the war. The chances to build on the emergency corporatism of wartime were lost. Lloyd George's own reputation as a social reformer and a friend of Labour was irreparably tarnished. Following Black Friday, the power of the unions was temporarily in abeyance, but in the years after 1918 Labour's political challenge to the regime of capitalist rule in government and industry had been immeasurably strengthened.

Labour's Political Advance, 1918–24

Given Henderson's ambitious plans, the actual results of the 1918 general election were disappointing for the Labour party. Labour fielded 361 candidates who between them polled two and a quarter million votes (20.8 per cent of the national total), but only 57 Labour MPs were elected.[24] The small increase over its pre-war strength was more than offset by the defeat of many of the party's leaders, including MacDonald, Snowden and Henderson.[25] The successful candidates were mostly trade union nominees, 25 of them miners from what were henceforth to be Labour's heartlands in the coalfields. The fact that Labour had come second in a further 79 seats was little comfort at a time when the 1918 Franchise Act had dramatically increased the size of the working class electorate and might have been expected to produce bigger gains. Labour's one real success was to have out-performed the Asquithian Liberal party, both in terms of seats and votes, to become numerically the main opposition to the Lloyd George government. But in the absence of its leaders from the Commons this was a hollow triumph. For the moment, the coalition of Conservatives and Lloyd George Liberals was overwhelmingly strong and Lloyd George, the 'Man Who Won The War', looked set to win the peace as well.

Yet, in one sense, Labour, or the Labour question, was already dominating the political scene. The industrial problems with which Lloyd George's government had to deal have already been described. In an influential study of *The Impact of Labour*,[26] Maurice Cowling has argued, on the basis of a detailed analysis of their private correspondence, that coalition politicians were preoccupied in the post-war period by the need to meet the Labour challenge on the political front too. The dimensions of that challenge had been obscured by the circumstances of the 1918 election – a snap election called to take advantage of the elevated patriotism engendered by the war and to capitalise on Lloyd George's personal popularity. But Labour soon began to make its electoral presence more strongly felt. It gained no fewer than fourteen seats at by-elections between 1918 and 1922, all from coalition candidates. While still far from being a truly national party, and with many unresolved organisational and policy difficulties to overcome, it was nonetheless at last showing the potential for growth that its supporters had hoped for and its opponents feared. At the 1922 election, held after the break-up of the coalition, Labour won 142 seats, polled 4.2 million votes (29.7 per cent of the total) and, with Ramsay MacDonald back at the helm following his return for Aberavon, was able to lay a more confident claim to the title of Official Opposition to the new Conservative government of Bonar Law.

The emergence of the Labour party, while it can be seen as a continuation of pre-war trends, was undoubtedly assisted by the upheavals of the First World War and by the calculations and confusion of its political opponents. The war had strengthened the institutional bases on which the Labour party relied for support, namely the trade unions and, to a lesser extent, the socialist societies. The experience of the war may have fostered a greater politicisation of the working class and made them more likely to support socialist or Labour candidates, a process of class identification encouraged by the economic and social unrest of the post-war period and by the failure of the 'businessmen's coalition' to fulfil its pledges of reconstruction and social reform. Yet while Labour got most of its support from working class voters, the working class as a whole did not automatically transfer its allegiance to Labour after 1918. 'Accidental' factors are therefore at least as important as sociological ones in explaining Labour's rise, and it is these that are increasingly being emphasised by historians who stress the limitations of Labour's post-war growth.[27]

The first of these factors was the split between the Asquithian and Lloyd Georgeite wings of the Liberal party which occurred as a result of the formation of the Lloyd George coalition in December 1916 and the decision of Lloyd George to perpetuate the coalition by means of the 'coupon' election in 1918. In that election, Asquith and his followers suffered a demoralising rout from which they recovered only slightly in 1922. Lloyd George's Coalition Liberals won 127 seats in 1918 largely by virtue of their freedom from Conservative opposition. In 1922, when those favourable arrangements no longer applied, their numbers were reduced drastically to 53, leaving Lloyd George as an ex-premier without a party.

The disintegration of the Liberal party created a political space into which the Labour party could move, taking over seats in the industrial areas and attracting middle class support from those Liberals disenchanted with the sorry state of their party in the post-war period.[28] Equally significant, though, in determining the scale and the timing of Labour's advance were the tactics of the Conservatives. In 1918 the Conservatives decided to maintain their alliance with Lloyd George because they thought, correctly as it turned out, that his aura of success would guarantee them a sweeping victory, defeating the Asquithians and holding back the Labour tide. By 1922, with Lloyd George's magic beginning to fade and the evidence of by-elections showing that Coalition Liberalism did not provide an effective bulwark against Labour's advance, their appraisal of the situation had altered. The threat from Labour no longer seemed as menacing as it had in the uncharted electoral territory of 1918. Although the Asquithian eclipse had created for Labour the unique opportunity of its being the sole viable challenger to the coalition, Labour's gains were less spectacular than might have been predicted. The Conservatives could therefore vote to end the coalition, confident in their ability to contain the challenge of Labour and win a majority in their own right, which they did.

There was still, perhaps, some slight chance that the Conservatives' bid for electoral supremacy could be foiled by the revival, in some form, of the pre-war progressive alliance between Labour and the Liberals. In November 1923, Stanley Baldwin, who had succeeded Bonar Law as Prime Minister in May, obtained a premature dissolution, ostensibly to seek a mandate from the voters for the introduction of protection. His real motive may have been to isolate Lloyd George and to destroy any lingering sympathy for 'coalitionism' within the Conservative party. This second aim was achieved, but only at a cost. The Conservatives lost their parliamentary majority, although they remained the largest single party, with 258 seats. However, the two wings of the Liberal party were reunited in defence of Free Trade and split the opposition vote almost evenly with Labour (4.3 million votes to Labour's 4.4 million). If the two non-Conservative parties could have combined again as they had before 1914 they would have had a solid working majority in the new House of Commons. Yet such was not to be. Even though their shares of the vote were nearly identical, Labour had a clear advantage in seats (191 to 158). MacDonald and his colleagues were unwilling to seek a coalition with a party they were attempting to replace as the main alternative to the Conservatives. A Liberal government was not feasible, though some Liberals thought that Asquith should have offered to form one. Asquith instead determined to help Labour to gain office by supporting a vote of no confidence in Baldwin, the Liberals remaining on the opposition benches. As a consequence of these manoeuvres, Ramsay MacDonald became Labour's first Prime Minister in January 1924.[29]

The first Labour government lasted only nine months, yet its impact on the politics of the 1920s was decisive. Brief though it was, the Labour ministers' tenure of office laid to rest the Churchillian jibe that Labour was not fit to govern. Nine months was also long enough finally to bury all hopes of resuscitating the progressive alliance. Liberal-Labour relations deteriorated steadily during the short parliament of 1924, the Liberals in the end allowing themselves to be forced into combining with the Conservatives to vote Labour out of office in sheer frustration at the humiliation of their position. The results of the 1924 election showed the cleverness of Baldwin's long-term strategy. At the expense of a short Labour government which had been unable because of its parliamentary position to enact any sweeping reforms he had created a situation in which the Conservatives could exploit hostility to a 'socialist' administration by using the 'red scare' tactics of the Campbell case and the Zinoviev letter [30] to put the squeeze on the Liberals. In a party system in which a Labour government was an established fact, the Conservatives could appeal to all non-Labour voters to vote Conservative in order to secure Labour's defeat. The Liberals, caught between an outworn progressivism and Baldwinite anti-socialism, had nothing to offer. In 1924 they lost over a hundred seats, returning a mere 40 MPs. Labour was turned out of office and the Conservative ascendancy which Baldwin had been striving for since 1922 was firmly established. Having been outmanoeuvred by the progressive parties before 1914, the Conservatives had at last gained their revenge in the complex, three-party politics of the 1920s.[31]

Two further things are worth noting about the Labour government of 1924, apart from the fact of its existence. One is the failure of Labour leaders to attempt, or even apparently to consider, any distinctive departures of policy. In part this derived from the ministry's minority status in parliament, dependent on Liberal support and Tory tolerance. Even so, there was a deeper conservatism to Labour's thinking which would probably have militated against the adoption of more radical policies in any event. For all the talk of 'socialism' and a 'New Social Order' Labour had developed no real plan for attaining its goals. It was pitchforked into office in 1924 before it was either intellectually or psychologically ready to govern in a socialist sense. MacDonald, despite his charismatic persona and his reputation as a theorist, was not a systematic reformer or a born administrator. His lack of government experience was a handicap which other ministers shared, and which forced him to augment his cabinet with late recruits to the Labour party like Lord Haldane, C. P. Trevelyan and Josiah Wedgwood from the Liberals and former Conservatives such as Lords Parmoor and Chelmsford. Yet their presence in the government was a reflection of Labour's lack of dynamism rather than a cause of it. Snowden, the Chancellor of the Exchequer and the former firebrand of the ILP, was reluctant to depart from the generally accepted canons of sound finance. His one concession to the Labour left was to allot an additional £28 million to provide relief works for the unemployed. MacDonald took the step of granting recognition to the Soviet Union, but this was a diplomatic rather than an ideological step. Even the much vaunted Wheatley Housing Act, introduced by the Clydeside ILP-er, John Wheatley, which offered subsidies for council house building, was little more than a revised version of the Housing Act passed by Lloyd George's government in 1919.[32]

The second aspect of the government's record which demands attention in the present context is its attitude towards trade union and industrial unrest. Liberals and Conservatives alike had warned that a Labour government would be a 'class' government, that it would represent a sectional interest rather than the community as a whole, because of its working class support and its trade union base. Leaving aside the obvious rejoinder that the Conservative and Liberal parties had offered a form of class government in the past, there seemed some substance to their fears. The trade unions provided the bulk of the Labour party's finance and much of its organisation. They helped to determine its policies through their block votes at the Labour party conference. Of the 191 Labour MPs in 1924, 101 were nominated by the trade unions.[33] Yet in fact, far from showing favouritism towards the unions, MacDonald's government went out of its way to demonstrate its even-handedness in industrial affairs, emphasising the importance of the community interest every bit as much as the New Liberals had before 1914. Its labour policy was scarcely different from that of Lloyd George or the Conservative administrations which had succeeded him, except for being couched in more brotherly language. Nor did the existence of a Labour government inhibit the trade unions in any way from pursuing their industrial ends. In February 1924 the London dockers embarked on a ten day strike for a two shillings a day increase in wages and an enquiry into the decasualisation of dock labour. In March, Bevin called a strike of London tramway workers and busmen, regardless of the fact that Harry Gosling, the TGWU President, was Minister of Transport in the MacDonald government.[34] In the latter case, when the rail unions threatened a sympathetic strike on the London Underground, the government invoked the 1920 Emergency Powers Act to protect essential services, for which they were criticised both by the TUC and by the Labour party's National Executive.

The events of 1924 thus provided reassurance for business and industrial interests that Labour could be trusted, at least temporarily, to govern without undue partiality. But while those outside the Labour movement greeted this discovery with relief, those on the inside were more frustrated than reassured. Labour supporters had not expected socialism overnight, certainly not from a minority government. They had expected a more determined attempt to stamp a Labour mark on office. Both on the left of the party and in the trade unions, the first Labour government was a chastening and disillusioning experience. The disillusionment which it left in its wake may have contributed more than a little to the mood of determination which produced the General Strike in May 1926.

The General Strike

The nine-day 'General Strike' of May 1926 was the climax of sixteen troubled years of industrial strife which had begun with the South Wales coal strike of 1910. As in the strike waves of 1910–12 and 1919–21 it was the problems of the coal industry that were its root cause. Since the late nineteenth century there had been bitter conflict between the owners and the unions. From the time of Rosebery's intervention in the dispute of 1893 the government had been increasingly involved as a third party, enacting legislation to limit hours and introduce minimum wages, and, during the First World War, taking control of the mines for the sake of the war effort. After 1918, as has been seen, the miners fiercely contested the government's decision to return the mines to private management and regarded the failure to act on the recommendations of the Sankey Commission as a betrayal by Lloyd George. Nor was the miners' sense of betrayal confined to the politicians, since they firmly believed also that they had been deserted by their allies in the Triple Alliance on the occasion of 'Black Friday' in April 1921. Left alone, they had been forced eventually to return to work on the owners' terms and to accept wage cuts in an attempt to maintain the profitability of their industry at a time of falling prices and post-war depression.

A partial recovery in the fortunes of the industry occurred in 1923 as a result of the French occupation of the Ruhr and the miners took advantage of this to negotiate an increase in wages in 1924. But the respite was short-lived. The long-term problems of the industry were severe, with increasing foreign competition, the loss of export markets and a declining domestic market as well. There was significant overmanning, the owners lacked capital for investment and many pits were working below their economic capacity. All of these difficulties were compounded by the decision of the Conservative government, in the person of its Chancellor of the Exchequer, Winston Churchill, to restore the Gold Standard in 1925, pegging the pound to its pre-war rates. Financially the aim was to return to 'normalcy' in the money markets and to safeguard London's position as a world financial centre, but for the country's export industries the effects were little short of disastrous, because they led to a substantial over-pricing of exports. Not surprisingly, once the French troops had withdrawn from the Ruhr and the artificial boom created by the cessation of German production had subsided, the coalowners were once again looking to cut their own production costs by reducing wages and increasing the hours of work. They gave notice that the 1924 agreement was to be terminated as from 31 July 1925.

The miners rejected the owners' terms and appealed to other unions for assistance, their case being strengthened by the feeling that the action of the coalowners might well be the prelude to a more general downward pressure on wages. They received support from the General Council of the TUC and from the transport workers and the railwaymen, upon whom the burden of any sympathetic action on the miners' behalf was likely to fall. The solidarity shattered in 1921 by Black Friday was restored. It was announced that the unions would impose an embargo on the movement of coal from 31 July if the owners' notices were not withdrawn and negotiations begun without preconditions. The threat of an embargo was sufficient to provoke an immediate conciliatory response from the Baldwin government. A temporary subsidy was offered to maintain wages at their existing levels and negotiations between employers and unions were to be shelved pending the report of a Royal Commission under the chairmanship of the Liberal politician and former Home Secretary, Herbert Samuel. This provided a basis for calling off the threatened industrial action and 'Red Friday' was widely hailed as a signal victory for the trade union movement.

But a final confrontation was only delayed, not avoided altogether. When the Samuel Commission reported in March 1926, it upheld the miners' arguments against lengthening hours but recommended a reorganisation of the industry which was likely to lead to job losses, and accepted that in the short term wage cuts might be necessary to maintain economic viability. Neither the mineowners nor the Miners' Federation were prepared to treat the report seriously, however; nor did the government take any steps to persuade them to do so. Instead the owners tried once again to impose their own settlement, announcing that when the government subsidy expired on 30 April they would revert to their 1925 plan for wage reductions and a return to district rather than national wage agreements. Again the miners, following their leaders Herbert Smith and A. J. Cook, rejected the owners' terms and called upon the TUC General Council for its support. The so-called 'General Strike' was the result.[35]

Even at this eleventh hour the members of the General Council were anxious to avoid any precipitate action and sought to reach a negotiated end to the dispute, doing their best to persuade the government to intervene with proposals of its own. At the same time, if a strike could not be averted the TUC leaders wanted to make sure that its conduct would be in their hands rather than those of the more implacable executive of the Miners' Federation. This was particularly a concern for those unions like the Transport Workers, whose members would be in the front line of a stoppage and who wanted to ensure that they were not drawn in to fighting for a lost cause. A conference of trade union executives held in London at the end of April gave the General Council the authority to handle the dispute on behalf of the movement as a whole and preparations for a sympathetic strike were set in motion, but every effort was still made to find a last minute solution. Hope was only finally abandoned when members of the General Council were told personally by Baldwin in Downing Street in the early hours of 3 May that negotiations were at an end. Strike action began on 4 May.[36]

The government's decision to break off negotiations when, according to trade union accounts, a settlement was in sight, was justified by Baldwin as a response to 'overt acts' which the unions themselves had taken, by which he meant the refusal of printers to produce copies of the *Daily Mail* unless an anti-union editorial was withdrawn. In reality, the government had been planning for a showdown with the unions for some time, preparations having begun after 'Red Friday' for measures to be taken in the event of a general strike. Sir John Anderson, a civil servant and future wartime cabinet minister, was placed in charge of these preparations and an unofficial Organisation for the Maintenance of Supplies had been set up. This is not to say that Baldwin wanted a strike, but some of his colleagues and supporters may have welcomed it as an opportunity to take on the unions and put them in their place. An element of brinkmanship may also have been present on both sides. Even so, the solidarity of the response which the TUC's strike call evoked was impressive. It has rightly been pointed out that the strike was not 'general', in the sense that not all the country's workers downed tools. The TUC plan was more selective, with groups such as the transport workers, printers and power workers being called out in the first phase and engineering and shipbuilding workers following a week later. But those groups called upon withdrew their labour almost to a man. On the railways, an estimated 99 per cent of workers went on strike; in London, buses, trams and the Underground came to a halt. Over a million and a half workers in addition to the one million miners joined the strike. For a stoppage improvised largely at the last moment by Bevin and one or two other leaders in the Strike Organisation Committee, it was a remarkable achievement, one which contained a warning for the government about the strength of working class support for their trade unions and about general working class dissatisfaction with the economic and political outlook.

Once the unions had demonstrated their capacity to organise a strike on this scale, the question for all concerned was how quickly and on what terms it could be brought to an end. Outwardly the government held firm, publishing its propaganda sheet, the *British Gazette* (edited by Churchill) and calling upon middle class volunteers to operate delivery and transport services. For the unions the worries were greater. The stoppage placed an enormous strain on union funds. There was the additional concern, either that solidarity would crumble if the dispute were prolonged or, conversely, that militants would seize control of the action for purposes of their own. Although the miners remained adamant in defence of their principle of

'Not a penny off the pay, not a second on the day', other union leaders were thus more willing to seek a compromise solution. When Sir Herbert Samuel offered to act as an intermediary his intervention was welcomed by the General Council and it was on the strength of a plan suggested by Samuel and apparently endorsed by the Prime Minister that the TUC agreed to call off the strike on 12 May.[37]

Any assessment of the General Strike turns first on the question of victory and defeat. Morally the unions had registered a great triumph. In practical terms, though, the laurels won by the General Council's negotiators soon turned to ashes. The Miners' Federation, whose leaders were absent from London and complained that they had not been consulted about the calling off of the strike, did not accept the Samuel plan as a basis for settlement and resolved to stay out. Their scepticism about the government's intentions was more than justified, as it transpired that Baldwin had not committed himself to securing the agreement of the owners to Samuel's proposals. Not only had the TUC failed, therefore, to settle the dispute which had caused the strike. They had also failed to secure guarantees that there would be no recriminations or victimisation of members of other unions who had taken part in sympathetic action. In the months that followed the end of the strike this came to be seen as a glaring omission. Many workers were required to submit to new terms of employment before returning to work; others were dismissed altogether. The government sided with the coalowners to the extent of reintroducing the statutory eight hour day in the mines in June 1926, in place of the seven hour day conceded in 1919. When the miners were finally starved into submission in October they also faced the certainty of wage cuts. Once again the unity of the trade union movement was fractured by the ineptitude and division of its leaders. The unions were soon, moreover, confronted with the threat of renewed curbs on their right to strike, in the form of the Trades Disputes Act of 1927.[38] Given the aftermath, any talk of victory for the unions in 1926 seems tragically misplaced.

The General Strike raised more profound questions about the place of Labour in British society and the extent of the gulf between the unions on the one hand and the employers and government on the other. Despite claims from some government supporters, sections of the press and legal experts such as Sir John Simon, there is no real case for arguing that the General Strike was illegal or unconstitutional. It was a stoppage of a sympathetic nature in furtherance of a trade dispute, not an attempt by the unions to overthrow the government or subvert the political institutions of the country. Nevertheless, as has been said, it did reveal the depth of divisions between capital and labour, not just in the mining industry but more generally across the economy as a whole. In many sectors of industry, it is true, systems of conciliation and collective bargaining were evolving in a satisfactory way, aided by the constructive statesmanship of Labour leaders like Ernest Bevin. But even there residues of bitterness and mistrust had accumulated, born out of the non-fulfilment of wartime pledges and the rising unemployment and falling wages of the depression years of the early 1920s. The attitude of employers was still all too often resistant to sharing the burdens of failing industries and too ready to squeeze wages in a desperate effort to sustain profits, or at least so it could easily appear to the miners, the dockers and others who suffered the sharp edge of the nation's economic decline.

Politically, the General Strike concentrated attention very much on the trade union aspect of the Labour question. The successful organisation of a national stoppage of work – even if it failed to achieve its objectives – was a terrific display of trade union power. Since the downfall of the Lloyd George coalition the attempt to integrate the unions into a more corporate structure of industrial relations and economic decision-making had been more or less abandoned. Conservative governments had tended to side with their natural supporters, the employers. Even the Labour government of 1924, with seven trade unionists in the cabinet, had done its best to keep the unions at arms length.[39] The lesson of this was not lost on the unions, who distanced themselves from the political leadership of the Labour movement after 1924 and ignored them during the General Strike. As W. J. Brown put it at the 1925 TUC, 'there was a permanent difference in point of view between the government on the one hand and the trade unions on the other . . . ', even if the government was a Labour one.[40] However, the General Strike illustrated the dangers of this difference becoming so pronounced that no common ground remained. The TUC were aware of the danger and did their best to prevent the breakdown of relations which a general strike implied. In the immediate aftermath of the strike government supporters were inclined to a triumphalist policy of limiting trade union rights. More far-sighted leaders – politicians, employers, trade unionists – were renewing the search for a less confrontational approach to relations between employers, workers and the state. Lloyd George had advocated conciliation during the General Strike itself. Afterwards others saw that the nation had been close to the brink and needed to take positive steps to avoid a repetition of the May days. In the early 1920s the Labour party had already been accommodated, after a fashion, into the political system. There was the possibility that the extremity which had been reached in 1926 might contain within it the seeds of a new settlement of the wider dimensions of the Labour question.

4

DEPRESSION AND INTEGRATION, 1926–45

Labour's alienation from the state did not end with the General Strike. It continued through the depression years of the 1930s and was arrested only by the changes in society and the economy that occurred in the Second World War. Even during the lifetime of the second Labour government of 1929–31 there was no fundamental reversal of attitudes; indeed, the crisis of 1931 which led to the formation of the National Government produced a confrontation between the political and trade union leaderships of the Labour movement more extreme, in its way, than that between the unions and the Baldwin government in 1926. Yet while on the surface the story of government-labour relations seems to be one of conflict and estrangement, in the 1920s and 1930s underlying trends were at work which laid the foundations for the more successful partnership between Labour and the state after 1939. This chapter accordingly examines the course of industrial politics in the late 1920s, the history of the Labour question in the 1930s and the forging of the wartime consensus of 1940–5, symbolised by the participation of the Labour party in Churchill's coalition government and the presence of Ernest Bevin, one of the leaders of the General Strike, as Churchill's Minister of Labour and National Service, with a seat in the War Cabinet.

Industrial Politics and the Second Labour Government

The 1920s saw the completion of the industrialisation of politics that had begun in the 1860s. This was evidenced by the prominence of economic and industrial issues – depression, unemployment, trade union power – in political debate. It was reflected too in changes in the party system. Before 1914, despite the Liberals' links with the Labour movement and the tendency of the Conservatives to act as a rallying point for commercial and business interests, the two major parties had remained basically middle class organisations, with more similarities than differences. After 1918, party politics showed a greater apparent divergence along class and industrial lines.[1] The Conservative party under the leadership of Bonar Law and Baldwin seemed to become unashamedly the party of the employers' interest, with a high proportion of business supporters and close ties with bodies such as the Federation of British Industries and the National Confederation of Employers' Organisations, formed in 1916 and 1919 respectively. The principal opposition, the Labour party, was equally clearly tied to the trade unions and representative of the interests of the industrial working class. The Liberals, who were the main victims of this process and who by the mid-1920s had shrunk to a third-party status with no institutional affiliations on either side of the industrial divide, appropriately enough staked their own claims to recovery on a programme of reconciling capital and labour by means of co-partnership, profit-sharing and improved industrial relations as outlined in the report of the Liberal Industrial Inquiry, *Britain's Industrial Future* (the so-called 'Yellow Book') in 1928.[2] For all parties, however, it was clear that industrial questions had ousted all but the most important topics of foreign policy as the leading items on the political agenda.

The close correlation between industrial and political divisions was illustrated by the controversy surrounding the Trades Disputes and Trade Union Act introduced by the Baldwin government in 1927. The General Strike had hardened the opinion of those in Tory ranks who believed that fresh curbs on the freedom of action of the trade unions were necessary, and these the 1927 Act set out to provide. It declared illegal all general strikes or sympathetic strikes designed to 'coerce the government either directly or by inflicting hardship on the community'.[3] The definition of 'intimidation' was tightened, to restrict the practice of picketing, and civil servants were prohibited from belonging to any TUC-affiliated union. At the same time, an attempt was made to reduce trade union financial support for the Labour party by substituting a provision for 'contracting in' in place of the existing practice of contracting out by members in regard to paying the political levy. Conservative party organisers conducted a sustained propaganda offensive to persuade the electorate of the necessity of these reforms.[4] Needless to say, the TUC and the Labour party took a sharply opposing view, denouncing the government's measure as partisan and vindictive and committing themselves to working for its eventual repeal.

However, while these differences were real enough, the pattern of industrial politics was evolving in more complicated and subtle ways than any simple capital-labour dichotomy of parties could explain. On occasion, certainly, the Conservative governments of the 1920s bowed to employers' pressure, as for instance in their repeated refusal to ratify the convention of the 1921 Washington conference in favour of a maximum 48 hour working week.[5] During the General Strike, the government had shown great deference throughout to the wishes of the coalowners, conceding their demand for the reintroduction of the eight hour day as well as giving them more general political backing. On the other hand, on an issue as important as the reform of trade union law, the unanimity between government and employers was far from complete. The most vociferous pressure for legislation came not from the government's 'capitalist' supporters but rather from backbench and constituency opinion. There is evidence that some ministers, including the Minister of Labour, Steel-Maitland, were opposed to the enactment of anything which could be interpreted as an 'anti-union' law, and the FBI and NCEO seem to have shared this more cautious and sceptical view. Indeed, they were devoting considerable effort in the wake of the General Strike to the task of opening up new channels of communication and co-operation with the trade unions and looked askance at anything which was likely to disrupt the search for an industrial rapprochement.

One instance of this attempt to find common ground between capital and labour was the series of informal 'Mond-Turner' talks between employers and members of the TUC General Council in 1928–9, begun on the initiative of Sir Alfred Mond, chairman of ICI, and Ben Turner and other TUC leaders. A second series of more formal discussions began in April 1929 involving representatives of the TUC, FBI and NCEO.[6] Although these had little practical result they did provide a valuable forum for the sharing of ideas on economic and industrial policy and were an important exercise in bridge-building after the conflicts of the earlier 1920s. They were an indication that the employers were beginning to see the unions more as partners in industrial enterprise than as enemies to be fought and excluded from all participation in decision making. The non-involvement of the government, despite Steel-Maitland's earlier hopes for industrial collaboration, demonstrated also that the structures of industrial politics could develop independently of, and to some extent transcend, the ritual conflict of the party-political sphere.

The politicians themselves were in any case not always in dia-metric opposition. While the issue of trade union law was obvi-ously divisive, on other questions some measure of agreement existed, at least about priorities for action. Unquestionably the most serious and persistent industrial problem of the 1920s was that of unemployment. After the collapse of the post-war boom in 1920, the level of unemployment had risen in 1921 to 17.1 per cent of the insured population. The total fell slightly thereafter as the worst of the slump receded, but it remained at ten per cent or above for most of the decade.[7] The reduction or relief of unemployment became a major preoccupation for politicians of all parties. Lloyd George's government had extended the unemployment insurance provisions in 1920 to cover all workers earning less than £250 a year, only to be forced into making cuts in benefit by the onset of the slump, when the rapid rise in the numbers of unemployed threatened to swamp the funds available for the scheme. The Labour government of 1924 raised the level of benefits again, but it was left to the Conservatives to attempt to recast the basis of the system of relief with their Unemployment Insurance Act of 1927.[8] Following the recommendations of the Blaneburgh Committee, this finally ended the pre-war concept of covenanted benefits, financed directly from an insurance fund, replacing them with 'standard' benefits (available to those who had paid the minimum thirty contributions in two years) and 'transitional' benefits for those who could not meet the '30 in 2' requirements. The only qualification for benefit was that the recipient must be 'genuinely seeking work'. If this test (originally introduced in 1921) could not be passed, benefit could be refused, as it was in as many as one in three cases in some areas.

Labour was critical of some aspects of the Conservative legislation, especially of the way in which the seeking work test was administered after 1927, and of the subsequent decision under the 1929 Local Government Act to replace the elected boards of Poor Law Guardians with Public Assistance Committees appointed by the local authorities, this last being a move by the government to prevent the spread of 'Poplarism', deriving from the practice of Labour Guardians in the London borough of Poplar of providing higher levels of unemployment benefit from the rates. Yet while there was disagreement over details, it was significant that the ultimate responsibility of the state for the welfare of the unemployed had been universally accepted. There was agreement too that unemployment was a by-product of the capitalist system and that any long-term reduction in the numbers of the unemployed would require a fundamental change in economic policy. The Conservatives favoured Protection, Baldwin talking guardedly in 1929 of 'safe-guarding' and imperial preference. Labour's preferred panacea was

'Socialism', which usually meant the nationalisation of basic industries and the improvement of welfare provision (the ILP argued in favour of a commitment to a 'Living Wage'). But neither of these long-term solutions represented practical politics in the 1920s, because of the electorate's continuing support for Free Trade and the lack of support for socialism. Only the Liberals were able to put forward an immediate plan for reviving the economy and dealing with the unemployment problem. Drawing upon the report of the Liberal Industrial Inquiry, in 1929 Lloyd George (who had led the party since 1926) offered voters the pledge of the 'Orange Book', *We Can Conquer Unemployment.*[9] His programme, influenced by the ideas of the Liberal economist John Maynard Keynes, proposed a carefully costed plan of 'National Development' and public works which would provide jobs for the unemployed and better roads, houses and infrastructural amenities for the community, regenerating the economy through increased public spending.

Whether the Liberal plan would have worked it is impossible to say. Notwithstanding that they had the most comprehensive industrial policy of any of the parties, the Liberals had lost the support of industrial working class voters. Despite a Liberal revival at by-elections in 1928–9, the party's underlying health was precarious and its unity under Lloyd George's leadership was strained. At the general election of 1929 the Liberals were unable to escape from their third party position. Their 513 candidates polled 5.3 million votes (23.6 per cent of the national total) but the electoral system rewarded them with only 59 seats.[10] Both MacDonald and Baldwin had portrayed the election as a straight fight between 'Capital and Labour' or Conservatism and 'Socialism' and the electorate seemed to share their analysis. With five million votes, the Liberals had not become quite the irrelevance that the other party leaders had hoped to make them, but Lloyd George's hopes of forming another government were dashed. Labour, with 287 seats to the Conservatives' 260, was the largest single party in the new parliament and Ramsay MacDonald was able to form his second minority administration.

If the 1929 election was a qualified victory for Labour over 'Capital', it is still necessary to exercise discretion in the transference of economic labels to the political system. As has been shown, the influence of employers over the Conservative party can be exaggerated, even if it is true that the party's policies tended to favour industry and the city rather than organised Labour. Similarly the experience of 1924 had demonstrated that a Labour government, though resting principally, if not exclusively, on working class support, was by no means a trade union government. By 1929 Labour was even less of a trade union party than it had been in 1924. Only six members of MacDonald's second cabinet were trade unionists, compared with seven in 1924. In 1929, for the first time, trade union nominated MPs were a minority of the parliamentary party (115 out of 287).[11] Even more dramatic was the electoral evidence of Labour's expansion beyond its trade union base. The crude figures need to be interpreted with care, but whereas in 1924 the totals of trade union members and Labour voters were numerically roughly equal, by 1929 the number of Labour voters (8.3 million) was almost double the total trade union membership (4.8 million) and more than double the affiliated membership of the TUC (3.7 million).[12] In order to establish itself as a governing party, Labour had had to win more marginal, less heavily unionised seats. MacDonald, while selectively using the rhetoric of socialism, had deliberately encouraged a 'national' rather than a 'class' image in order to attract middle class and non-union voters, thus enabling Labour to appeal more readily to the Liberals' former radical constituency.

Partly for this reason, the industrialisation of politics which had produced the second Labour government also made it especially vulnerable. Its position, though stronger than in 1924, was still a minority one, dependent upon at least the tacit support of one or other of the opposition parties. Because of its aspirations towards 'Socialism' it was viewed with suspicion by industrial and business interests, yet in trying to appease their concerns it risked trouble with its own left wing (the ILP) and with the trade unions. Added to this it was unfortunate in the timing of its assumption of office. In October 1929 the Wall

Street crash signalled the intensification of the international depression. Unemployment, which had stood at 1.2 million in June 1929 when Labour came to power, had reached 2.5 million by December 1930. In an era when governments were coming to be judged more by economic criteria than by any other factors, this was a stern test of Labour's capacity for effective action.[13]

The government's response to the worsening economic situation was to set in motion a number of enquiries. The Macmillan Committee on Finance and Industry was appointed in November 1929, with Keynes and Ernest Bevin among its members. J. H. Thomas, the former railwaymen's leader who became Lord Privy Seal, was appointed to chair a special ministerial committee on unemployment, the other members of which were George Lansbury, a veteran of the Poplar Guardians' struggles of the 1920s, Thomas Johnston, the under secretary of state for Scotland, and the inventive and aristocratic Sir Oswald Mosley. In January 1930 MacDonald took the further step of setting up an Economic Advisory Council to discuss economic problems. He also attempted to involve the opposition parties in the search for a solution to the nation's difficulties, inviting them to consider the House of Commons as a 'Council of State' in which partisan differences might be put aside and, in May 1930, issuing a formal invitation to the Conservative and Liberal leaders to take part in 'conversations' with the government.

It is customary to interpret these moves as a sign of weakness and to criticise the Labour government for its inadequacy and inaction in dealing with the mounting economic crisis. Snowden's fierce attachment as Chancellor to what he considered the principles of fiscal rectitude ruled out any major spending initiatives such as those contained in the Liberal programme of 1929 or hinted at in Labour's own manifesto, *Labour and the Nation*. When Oswald Mosley, frustrated by the lack of urgency in the government's unemployment policy, produced his personal Memorandum advocating more rigorous economic controls this was shelved by the cabinet and rejected by the parliamentary party, precipitating Mosley's resignation and his eventual departure to found the New Party in 1931.

In the summer of 1930, following MacDonald's invitation to the opposition parties, the government began discussions with Lloyd George on the possibility of Liberal support for a programme of unemployment relief works and land reform, but these achieved little, partly because of the advanced state of disintegration of the Liberal party by this time, partly because of MacDonald's suspicion of Lloyd George.[14] Faced with the crisis of capitalism which they had long predicted, Labour ministers seemed helpless in the grip of events beyond their control.

To some extent they were, as any other government would have been. Yet Labour's alleged shortcomings need to be kept in perspective. Until the summer of 1931 they were pursuing a course that was at least keeping the economy on an even keel, and MacDonald's overtures to the opposition were a constructive, if necessary, response to an unusual political situation. It can be argued that more imaginative schemes of public enterprise could have been attempted to boost the economy, but there is no guarantee that, even if these had been politically feasible, they would have achieved the results that their advocates, either then or since, have claimed.[15] In any case, the Labour leaders can hardly be blamed for being influenced by the weight of economic orthodoxy which stressed the importance of balanced budgets and by the need to maintain both the confidence of financial institutions and of the opposition in parliament, which, Lloyd George apart, was mostly in favour of reductions in spending rather than the reverse. The long-term problems of British industry were not of Labour's making and it was unrealistic to expect MacDonald and his colleagues to come up with instant solutions when more strongly placed governments of other parties had failed to do so in the past.

Nevertheless, the government's failure to act more decisively sharpened tensions within the Labour movement. There had already been criticism from the unions of the limitations of the Coal Mines Bill introduced in December 1929, which provided for a reduction in the working day from eight to seven-and-a-half hours rather than the seven hours the miners wanted and which was seen by the left as giving too many concessions to the owners. Lloyd George's attacks on the government for its conservative policies on the coal industry and on unemployment acted as an additional irritant. Further disappointment came when an attempt to repeal the 1927 Trade Disputes Act had to be abandoned because of Conservative and Liberal opposition. But it was the government's attitude on the wider economic front that caused the greatest union concern. In February 1931 ministers agreed to the appointment of the May Committee to investigate the possibility of reductions in public expenditure. When the Committee reported at the end of July it recommended £96 million of spending cuts and £24 million in extra taxation to cover a predicted budget deficit of £120 million. Before the Cabinet Economic Committee had met to consider these proposals, which included a 20 per cent reduction in the level of unemployment benefit, a series of banking collapses in Austria and Germany had triggered a crisis of confidence in which there were fears of a serious run on the pound if measures were not taken at once to implement the May Committee recommendations.

The full ramifications of the crisis cannot be considered in detail here.[16] Its handling by the government was politically maladroit, however, and its significance for the Labour movement was twofold. First it led to an open split between Labour ministers and the TUC General Council. If there had been fuller consultations between government and unions at an earlier stage, this might perhaps have been avoided, but when MacDonald and Snowden finally met the General Council on 20 August it was too late for a compromise. TUC leaders rejected the proposed emergency package and flatly refused to accept the need for cuts in unemployment benefit. Bevin, indeed, using his intuitive understanding of the economy and the knowledge gained from membership of the Macmillan Committee, strongly urged an alternative to the deflationary programme to which the government, the opposition parties and the financial experts were all committed.[17] Although his views made little impression on either the Prime Minister or the Chancellor, his advocacy was powerful enough to win over Arthur Henderson and to provoke dissent in the cabinet. This led to the second consequence of the crisis, the collapse of the Labour government itself. Unable to gain the full agreement of his colleagues to the proposed cuts, MacDonald tendered his resignation to the King. On 24 August he accepted a personal commission to form a 'National Government' with the Conservative and Liberal parties, leaving most of his erstwhile Labour colleagues to take themselves into opposition under Henderson's leadership. At a critical moment in the economic history of the inter-war period, the Labour movement had lost the political protection of a Labour government and was once more at the mercy of a Conservative-dominated coalition.

The Labour Question in the 1930s

Labour denounced the formation of the National Government as a 'bankers' ramp'. MacDonald, Snowden and Thomas, the Labour ministers who joined the National cabinet, were branded as traitors and expelled from the party. The charges of betrayal were probably misplaced.[18] MacDonald had not carried out a calculated deception intended to secure his own continuance in office at the expense of his party. He was convinced that a coalition government would have a better chance than a purely party-based administration of carrying the measures necessary to restore confidence, and that it was his duty to serve as its head. But he saw this as no more than a temporary expedient, after which normal party warfare, and his own leadership of the Labour party, could be resumed. The Conservatives had other ideas. After the National Government had been forced to take Britain off the Gold Standard in September 1931 (one of the eventualities, ironically, which its formation had been supposed to prevent), Conservative ministers began to press MacDonald to call a general election to procure a 'doctor's mandate' for the coalition to take whatever measures were necessary to revive the country's economic fortunes. MacDonald's expulsion from the Labour party gave him no reason to resist this pressure and the election duly took place in October, with MacDonald and Snowden launching a bitter onslaught on the irresponsibility of their former Labour colleagues and Snowden intemperately dismissing the programme of the Labour opposition as 'Bolshevism run mad'. In this highly charged atmosphere Labour suffered a defeat as crushing as that which the Asquithian Liberals had experienced in 1918. The coalition parties (Conservatives, Liberals and MacDonald's 'National Labour' group) were returned to power with a total of 554 seats. The Labour party registered a net loss of about two million votes compared with 1929 and won a mere 46 seats.[19] Most of its leaders, including Henderson, were defeated, only George Lansbury, Clement Attlee and Stafford Cripps being among the survivors.

The crisis of 1931 and its denouement created a new context for the Labour question in the 1930s. Politically, the Labour question had for the time being almost ceased to exist. Since 1906, the aim of the non-Labour parties – first the Liberals, then the Conservatives – had been to contain Labour's rise. This had been a prime motive of the coalition government of 1918–22, as it was of Baldwin's exploitation of fears of socialism in 1924 which he had used not merely to defeat Labour but to destroy the Liberals as well. In 1931 Baldwin was given a further opportunity to perpetuate the Conservatives' dominance of inter-war politics at the expense of their rivals. MacDonald was detached from the Labour party and manoeuvred into calling an election. The Conservatives increased their representation from 260 MPs to 470, giving them an absolute majority in their own right and leaving the 'National' label of the government as little more than a polite fiction to disguise the scale of their victory. Labour might well have lost an election in 1931 even it it had fought as a united party, but the circumstances of the contest made its defeat more sweeping than it would otherwise have been. The 'forward march' which the Labour party had been making since 1918 was decisively halted. There was a slight Labour recovery at the election of 1935, when Labour won 154 seats to the coalition's 429, but it presented no serious threat to the government for the remainder of the decade.

Labour's industrial challenge was similarly less pronounced. The government still had serious industrial problems with which to deal, of which unemployment remained the most acute. The Communist-backed National Unemployed Workers' Movement flourished briefly during the depression years of the early and mid-1930s; there were clashes between its members and the police and leaders like Sid Elias and Wal Hannington were arrested.[20] But the NUWM received no official support from the TUC and the kind of widespread industrial disturbances that had taken place in the 1920s, with the massive deployment of troops and police, did not recur in the 1930s. For the first part of the decade trade union membership was in decline, as it had been since the mid-1920s, and members were more concerned with preserving jobs than with large-scale agitation. Militancy had received a setback during the General Strike of 1926 and the unions were operating under the more restrictive conditions of the 1927 Trades Disputes Act. The 1930s were accordingly, in the words of one recent writer, 'a decade of sullen industrial peace'.[21] The unions attempted to compensate for their diminishing industrial power by effecting a rapprochement with the political organisation of the Labour party, though this had only a limited impact on the political-industrial scene before the outbreak of the Second World War.

Economically, the Thirties may be characterised as a decade of 'Boom and Gloom'. Gloom there was aplenty. Unemployment continued to rise after 1931, peaking at 2,745,000 in 1932. It fell slightly, with fluctuations, thereafter, but there were still over a million and a half unemployed in 1939. In areas like South Wales and the North of England, and in the depressed heavy industries such as coalmining, steel-making and shipbuilding, the concentrations of unemployment were particularly high. One calculation estimates that in the depth of the depression in 1931–2 as many as 35 per cent of miners, 48 per cent of steel workers and 62 per cent of shipbuilding employees were out of work.[22] 'Hunger Marches' from places like Jarrow and South Wales to London became enduring images of the depression years. Against these, however, there has to be set a more prosperous side of the picture. While the old staple heavy industries were in decline, newer industries – car manufacturing, chemicals, electrical engineering – were growing up in the Midlands and the South-East of England. For those in work, there was a rise in real incomes and a feeling of increasing prosperity. Much of the industrial growth of the 1930s was fuelled by a domestic consumer boom which had a further knock-on effect, creating new jobs and stimulating the building and construction industries. In the midst of depression, a new industrial England (if not yet a new Scotland or a new Wales) was being born – a fact which helps to explain the electoral success of the National Government and which had its own implications for the future of the Labour question.[23]

The shifting economic balance brought changes both in the composition and the outlook of the trade union movement. Trade union membership fell to an inter-war low in 1933, at 4.3 million, of whom 3.2 million were in unions affiliated to the TUC. The figures had recovered by 1939 to a total of 6.3 million, 4.8 million in TUC-affiliated unions.[24] The density of trade union membership (that is, the proportion of the workforce which belonged to trade unions) rose from 27.4 per cent in 1933 to 37.8 per cent in 1938, regaining the level last attained in 1925.[25] However, the overall statistics conceal some important internal movements. The Miners' Federation, for example, lost members throughout the 1930s, declining from 804,236 in 1929 to 588,321 in 1939. This was due in part to the loss of members to the breakaway 'Spencer' union in Nottinghamshire, but mainly to the effects of the depression. Although mining remained highly unionised, it was a shrinking industry. The same was true of other stalwarts of the Labour movement such as the textile unions. Meanwhile, those unions which recruited members in previously unorganised sectors of the economy, or in the new industries, were undergoing rapid expansion, accounting for most of the increase in total trade union membership by the end of the decade. The Amalgamated Engineering Union doubled its membership to about 400,000 between 1933 and 1939. The big 'general' unions achieved similar success. The General and Municipal Workers expanded from 269,357 members in 1934 to 467,318 in 1939. Ernest Bevin's TGWU had 654,510 members by 1937, not only replacing the miners as the largest union in the TUC but becoming the largest union in the world.[26]

These changes had important repercussions within the TUC. The influence of moderates like Bevin increased while that of the militants, in the Miners' Federation and elsewhere, waned. This confirmed the trend towards a more realistic, professional approach to industrial affairs which had been the hallmark of TUC policy since the failure of the General Strike in 1926. Apart from Bevin, the chief architect of this approach was Walter Citrine, who had become acting General Secretary of the TUC in 1925 and took over the post on a permanent basis in the following year. The Bevin-Citrine axis was the decisive influence in TUC politics throughout the late 1920s and 1930s. They realised the barrenness and ultimate self-destructiveness of the confrontational stance adopted by the miners towards owners and government alike and tried to develop a more constructive policy. The Mond-Turner talks and the discussions with the FBI and NCEO in 1928–9 were the first fruits of this change of heart. Their willingness to co-operate with the government was demonstrated by Bevin's membership of the Macmillan Committee and of MacDonald's Economic Advisory Council, of which Citrine was also a member. The crisis of 1931 cut short the experiment of co-operation at this level but the setback was not accepted as final. The TUC's Economic Committee, set up in 1928, continued to develop its own policies and to initiate research projects conducted by an enlarged full-time secretariat. The unions also acted to increase their influence over the Labour party, so that the divisive split of 1931 could not be repeated. On Citrine's initiative, the National Joint Council of the Labour movement was remodelled to give the TUC General Council increased representation *vis-à-vis* the party's National Executive and the parliamentary Labour party, and the TUC staked its claim to 'initiate and participate in any political matter which it deems to be of direct concern to its constituents'.[27] Not only was this designed to create greater unity in the political and industrial leadership of the Labour movement. For the unions, securing influence over the Labour party was the first step to securing influence over a future Labour government and so to broadening the field of trade union action in the political sphere.

The concomitant of a less confrontational policy was the avoidance of large scale conflict in the industrial arena. The 1930s were one of the quietest decades on record as far as industrial relations were concerned, both in terms of the number of stoppages and the aggregate of days lost due to industrial action.[28] Union leaders were quick to crack down on unofficial disputes initiated by the rank-and-file, especially where these owed something to Communist infiltration, as in the case of the London busmen which plagued Bevin's TGWU in this period. The Bevin-Citrine leadership of the TUC was criticised by the left for its 'Mondist' approach and for not campaigning more vigorously on behalf of the unemployed, but these criticisms did not always take account of the environment in which the unions were operating or of the fact that they had to represent the interests of the prosperous as well as the depressed areas. The loss of membership due to depression necessitated a period of retrenchment, while it took time to consolidate a position in the more rapidly growing sectors of the economy. Employers there were often resistant to union penetration and had to be won over by a demonstration of restraint. Neither the resources of the unions nor the general economic situation were conducive to precipitate strike action. The main emphasis of activity, therefore, was on gaining recognition for the unions in the new industries and carrying on the painstaking work of building up collective bargaining procedures. Bevin and the TGWU in particular had been working for the establishment of joint industrial councils since the early 1920s, and in many cases these were remarkably successful in providing a negotiating forum in which employers and unions could reach agreement on wages and conditions in the interests of the industry as a whole. The flour-milling industry, for example, which had a JIC, did not have a single strike throughout the inter-war period.[29]

As individual unions tried to impose greater discipline on their members, the TUC General Council, in addition to its other roles, became more active in resolving disputes between unions, especially those that arose as unions competed for members in the expanding or diversifying newer industries. The 'Bridlington Agreement' adopted by the TUC at its annual meeting in 1939 established clear guidelines for recruitment, member unions agreeing not to organise in a plant or industry in which another union already represented a majority of the workforce. The General Council was empowered to arbitrate in inter-union disputes, in a similar way to that in which the Board of Trade and the Ministry of Labour had earlier assumed powers to offer conciliation in disputes between unions and employers.

In contrast with earlier periods, the government was less involved in the settlement of disputes than it had been in the 1920s or before 1914. With employers and unions successfully regulating their own affairs, ministers played little or no part in wage bargaining in the private sector, although they took a much closer interest in public sector negotiations. The state continued to enact protective legislation governing working conditions, as in the Shops Act (1934), the Factory Act (1937) and the Holidays with Pay Act (1938). But even more than in the 1920s the government's main concern was for those who were out of work rather than for those who were fully employed. The Unemployment Act of 1934 restored the level of benefits reduced in 1931 and introduced further changes in the administration of unemployment relief, including the establishment of Unemployment Assistance Boards. Measures were also introduced by the National Government to respond to the particular needs of the depressed areas. The Special Areas (Development and Improvement) Act of 1934 appointed special commissioners to encourage the development of new industries in the single-industry districts where unemployment was highest. A further measure in 1937 provided tax concessions for employers willing to locate plants in depressed areas. Although not especially successful (and more than vitiated in their usefulness as an electoral ploy by the continuance of the hated 'Means Test' imposed as a qualification for individual assistance for the unemployed), these Acts marked the tentative beginnings of a regional industrial policy which went beyond anything that governments had previously attempted.[30]

The Special Areas legislation was part of a gathering debate about the involvement of government in economic and industrial planning in the 1930s. The National Governments after 1931 embarked upon what in the context of the time was an adventurous programme of 'rationalisation', building on earlier measures of state intervention such as the railway grouping of 1921, the creation of the national electricity grid in 1926 and the Coal Mines Act of 1930. Having introduced measures of tariff protection in 1932, the government gave its assistance to the depressed industries like coal, textiles, steel and shipbuilding to encourage them to reduce overcapacity and to adopt more efficient production methods. This was the motive behind support for the establishment of the British Iron and Steel Federation in 1936 and the passage of the Cotton Industry Reorganisation Act of 1938, which offered subsidies to compensate for lost capacity. Mining royalties were nationalised in 1938 to provide a fund to finance reorganisation in the coal industry. In the food distribution industry, a number of agricultural marketing boards were set up (including those for milk and potatoes in 1933) to market produce on a more co-operative, large-scale basis; the Sugar Industry Reorganisation Act of 1935 grouped sugar refining under the aegis of the British Sugar Corporation. In most cases ownership remained vested in private hands. It was nevertheless significant that even a predominantly Conservative government should be convinced by the state of Britain's industry of the need for more economic planning and a greater degree of government intervention, including the funding of more intensive scientific research.[31]

While the government was engaged in these experiments in rationalisation, the opposition parties were reviewing or recasting their own economic and industrial policies. The Liberals made less of a contribution to the economic debate in the 1930s than they had in the 1920s. The Simonite Liberal Nationals, who remained in the National Government, followed the Conservative line, protection included. The official Liberal party, led by Herbert Samuel until 1935 and by Sir Archibald Sinclair thereafter, resigned from the National Government in 1932 in protest against the decision to implement a tariff policy but their main preoccupation was their own political survival and they lacked the impetus of innovative economic thinking following their breach with Lloyd George in 1931. Lloyd George himself, having denounced the National Government as loudly as did its Labour critics, continued to advocate his 'New Deal' policies, encouraged by the success of Roosevelt in the United States and, up to a point, of Hitler in Germany, as well as by support from younger Conservatives like Harold Macmillan.[32] At the 1935 election Lloyd George sponsored a 'Council of Action' as an alternative to the National Government, with economic policies similar to those of 1929. By then, however, he was a declining force, as was the other innovative figure of the 1929–31 period, Sir Oswald Mosley.[33] Mosley's New Party had foundered at the 1931 election, winning no seats. Mosley was pushed further and further towards a fascist solution to economic and social problems, launching the British Union of Fascists in 1932. There was still some originality in his corporatist economic thinking, but this could not outweigh the unappealing nature of his movement as a whole, and neither autarky nor anti-semitism proved to be a passport to electoral success.

For an alternative economic policy the electorate had really to look to the Labour party. There were signs in the 1930s that Labour was genuinely trying to put its house in order after the debacle of 1931. Let down in a crisis by intellectual vagueness and their lack of economic expertise, Labour politicians and trade unionists began to think more coherently about what Labour's economic programme should be and how it was to be implemented. The disaffiliation of the ILP in 1932 deprived Labour of one source of ideas (and they rejected outright any alliance with the Communists), but others were provided by the setting up of the New Fabian Research Bureau and the Society for Socialist Inquiry and Propaganda. The party conference discussed proposals for the nationalisation of basic industries in 1932–3, with Herbert Morrison's plan for public corporations on the lines of the London Passenger Transport Board winning the day despite trade union misgivings about the absence of workers' representation on such bodies. In some ways the debate became rather sterile in the mid-1930s, partly because there was no immediate prospect of power, also because it was diverted by Cripps and others into a discussion of the need for a Labour government to introduce emergency legislation to circumvent the vested interests of the financial world and the House of Lords. By 1937, however, an agreement on priorities had been reached and Labour's commitment to parliamentary democracy confirmed, making the party more electable and providing a partial blueprint for the policies of the Attlee administration after 1945.

In the late 1930s, a Labour government was still some way in the future and the Labour question was receding in the public mind as the deteriorating international situation became the main focus of concern. Yet in reality the two issues were not unconnected. The Labour movement shared the mounting apprehension produced by the aggression of Mussolini and Hitler and by the events of the civil war in Spain. Trade unionists and socialists in Britain were in some respects more aware of what was happening on the continent than were the members of the British government, having seen, as they had, the suppression of trade union and social democratic movements in Germany, Austria and Czechoslovakia. Union leaders like Ernest Bevin played a major part in shaping the Labour party's foreign policy towards support for collective security and rearmament, a process epitomised by Bevin's famous attack on the pacifist George Lansbury at the 1935 Labour party conference, which led to Lansbury's resignation as leader and his replacement by Attlee just before the 1935 election.

More than that, the approach of war made the Labour question a matter of greater rather than lesser importance for the country as a whole. A second European war in a generation would draw even more heavily upon the nation's economic and industrial resources than that of 1914–18 had done, and the need for co-operation between the government and organised Labour would be even more pressing. It was noticeable that whereas there had been comparatively little consultation between government and unions in the 1930s, in 1938–9 the unions were drawn into discussions by ministers on a wide range of questions connected with plans for mobilisation and civil defence. When war broke out in 1939 the immediate involvement of union leaders and Labour politicians in war work was limited. But the *laissez faire* attitude of Chamberlain's government could not last, and, as will be seen, when Churchill became Prime Minister in May 1940 the war in which Britain was involved became Labour's war as well.

The Wartime Consensus, 1940–5

The lessening of tension that surrounded the Labour question in the 1930s was based on a series of largely negative factors: the weakening of organised Labour by the effects of depression; the adoption of a less aggressive attitude on the part of the employers; and the virtual withdrawal of government from the conduct of industrial relations. Some writers have discerned a developing triangular relationship between the three agencies; Bevin talked of the unions in 1937 as an integral part of the state. Yet it was too early to say that the alienation of Labour from the institutions of government had been completely reversed, even if relations between the political and industrial leadership of the Labour movement had improved after 1931 and if the Baldwin and Chamberlain governments showed a greater willingness, or a lessening reluctance, to consult the unions on matters of policy. The unions were still jealous of their independence. They and the employers' organisations may have taken on what Middlemas describes as the 'corporate bias' of 'governing institutions',[34] but no fully corporate relationship between unions, employers and the state had evolved.[35]

Between 1940 and 1945 something like a revolution occurred in the relations between Labour and the state. Labour's part-nership, on the basis of 'moral equality'[36] if not numerical parity, with the Conservatives in the Churchill coalition, and in particular Bevin's appointment as Minister of Labour in May 1940, were the prelude to far-reaching changes in the position and status of the Labour movement, in relations between industry and government and ideas about social and industrial policy, and in the political prospects of the Labour party. The resulting mix of assumptions, policies and relationships is often described as an essential part of the wartime consensus.[37] For a study of the politics of the Labour question, two crucial questions emerge. How deep was this consensus, supposing it existed? How easily could the pattern of wartime co-operation be transferred to the different conditions that would pertain once the war was won?

In order to answer these questions it is necessary first to look at some of the practical effects of the war itself. As in the First World War, the key problems on the domestic front were mobilisation and manpower. Military conscription was introduced at an earlier stage than in the previous war and the Emergency Powers Act of 1940 gave the Ministry of Labour and National Service considerable freedom in the direction of labour, but it was still necessary for large armies to be assembled almost from scratch without depriving industry of the skilled workers who would be needed for the expansion of the munitions industries and other aspects of war production. Given the vital nature of these tasks, the appointment of Ernest Bevin was as significant as any that Churchill made during the entire war.[38] Bevin had made his reputation as a trade union leader, not as a politician. He had to be found a seat in parliament on taking office (although he had unsuccessfully contested the elections of 1918 and 1931). But unlike the trade union Ministers of Labour in the First World War, his personal authority was immense and he had the confidence and the scope to use it to the full. During his term of office the Ministry of Labour greatly extended its organisation and its functions until it became arguably the most important department on the Home Front. Next to Churchill, Bevin was seen by many as the government's most powerful and respected member.

Bevin was determined from the outset to proceed as far as possible by means of co-operation rather than compulsion. At a meeting with trade union executives at the Central Hall, Westminster, on 21 May 1940 he explained the war situation and secured union approval for his immediate plans. A Joint Consultative Committee of employers and trade unionists was established to advise on the direction and implementation of policy. Negotiations were carried on with the unions most closely affected by the introduction of measures for the dilution and redeployment of skilled labour so as to make optimum use of scarce resources. Yet an element of compulsion was inseparable from the process of mobilisation, even if it was willingly accepted. Essential Work Orders were used to register skilled workers and to direct them to where they were most needed. A manpower budget was devised to allocate available labour between the armed services and jobs in home industry, or between differently prioritised programmes of war production. To meet successive labour shortages as the war progressed an increasingly draconian range of expedients had to be resorted to, including, finally, the conscription of women for war work. Although the unions were consulted at every stage in this process, their interests had inevitably to be subordinated to the demands of the total war effort, which, at the peak of mobilisation in 1943–4, had drawn in something like two-thirds of the adult population, many of them not even union members, either to serve in the armed forces or to undertake war-related work on the domestic front.

It was a tribute to Bevin's sensitive handling of labour problems, and perhaps even more to the sense of common purpose produced by the war, that the direction of labour on this scale did not provoke greater unrest in industrial relations. True, under Order in Council 1305 strikes and lock-outs were officially banned for the duration of the war and a National Arbitration Tribunal was set up to impose compulsory settlements, but Bevin was reluctant to initiate prosecutions of strikers and for the most part Order 1305 remained a dead letter.[39] Normal collective bargaining procedures continued to operate where these were in place and no strict limits were imposed on wage rises, despite Treasury pressure for a firmer policy. Where collective bargaining was weak the government intervened to increase wages among the low-paid, as in the case of agricultural workers in 1941. Otherwise the unions were urged to show restraint in their claims at a time when labour was in short supply and to raise earnings by increasing productivity. On the whole the policy of preserving voluntarism was a successful one. The number of strikes and stoppages did increase as the war went on, and was generally higher than during the First World War or in the 1930s, but the duration of most strikes was short and the total of days lost small in relation to the numbers of men and women employed.[40] Only in the coal industry was there a serious underlying level of discontent which threatened war production, although there were strikes too in the engineering trades, the transport industry and the docks at various stages in the war.

It is difficult to make assessments of the wartime standard of living. For most of the war wages rose faster than prices and earnings were boosted by overtime and special payments. With the demand for manpower, work was plentiful and unemployment virtually disappeared. On the other hand, life was undoubtedly hard, with rationing, consumer shortages and physical danger, as well as the mental and emotional stress inseparable from a major military conflict. At least in terms of labour conditions, though, Bevin did all he could to lessen the hardships of workers whose pattern of life had been disrupted and who were sometimes working in a strange and hostile environment. He used the powers of the Ministry of Labour to effect a number of reforms, some of which survived the war. Under the Essential Work Orders employers were required to provide a certain minimum standard of comfort for their workers. Not only did safety regulations have to be observed and fair wages paid, works canteens, medical facilities and other amenities had also to be provided. The Ministry of Labour took over responsibility for factory inspection from the Home Office to ensure that these conditions were met. Ministry of Labour officials offered assistance to workers transferred away from their home areas and a new industrial welfare system was thus created. Other measures included training for the disabled and guarantees of educational provision for those forced to terminate full-time schooling because of the war. The Factory and Welfare Division of the Ministry of Labour became a kind of social service state in embryo. In addition, a sustained attempt was made to end the problems of low pay. Forty-six new Wages Boards were set up between 1940 and 1945 and given permanent form by the Wage Councils Act of 1945. The Catering Wages Act of 1943, carried against considerable backbench Conservative opposition, extended state regulation to a previously unorganised, low-wage industry and was another example of the way in which the war had forced the pace of government intervention in the regulation of working conditions.

Of course, Bevin's welfare measures were only a reflection of the quickening interest in social policy generated by the war and by thoughts of post-war reconstruction. There was a general agreement, both in the government and outside, that the mistakes of 1918–22 should not be allowed to repeat themselves and that the collective energy which the war had unleashed should be used to effect a permanent improvement in the quality of life of all classes of the population. The Beveridge Report on social insurance, published in December 1942 at a turning point in the war and immediately a bestseller, captured the national mood.[41] Churchill was initially reluctant to become involved in a discussion of post-war policy which might open up divisions in the coalition and divert attention from the overriding objective of defeating Hitler. By 1944, however, reconstruction plans were well advanced. The Butler Education Act was placed on the statute book, promising secondary education for all. An important series of White Papers were published which outlined the shape of a future 'welfare state', including a comprehensive scheme of *Social Insurance* (September 1944), *A National Health Service* (February 1944) and, crucially, the commitment to the maintenance of full employment in the White Paper on *Employment Policy* (May 1944). This last prefigured a drastic departure from pre-war practice, when governments had acted to relieve the unemployed but not to manage the economy in such a way as to ensure work for all. The implication was clearly that the state would become not only the provider of welfare services for its citizens but that the economy would somehow be managed for the social good rather than for the enrichment of a narrow class of capitalists and entrepreneurs.

The idea of a managed economy presupposed some alterations in the running, and possibly the ownership, of industry. During the war basic industries had again been brought under state control, as they had between 1914 and 1918. The government had worked with unions and management to set targets and production quotas, to assign labour and raw materials and to ensure the harmonisation of different sections of the economy in the national interest. It seemed logical that planning of this sort should be continued into the peace, thus avoiding the conflict and dislocation which had resulted from the rush to 'decontrol' industries after the First World War. Indeed, one of the chief legacies of the wartime experience was an acceptance of the need for greater state control in many areas of industrial life, and employers and trade unionists could envisage working closely with government departments on a more permanent basis. The concept of a 'mixed' economy, in which certain functions were undertaken by the state and the rest by private enterprise working within carefully-defined parameters, gained increasing support.[42]

To what extent did this amount to a 'consensus', operating across party-political and industrial boundaries? The broad features of the welfare programme that was to be the centrepiece of social reconstruction were agreed within the coalition and by public opinion outside. The experience which the Treasury had gained in operating Keynesian tools of economic management suggested that the White Paper aim of maintaining 'a high and stable level of employment' was attainable, particularly if predictions of post-war labour shortages were borne out, although it was a political hostage to fortune which Conservative politicians especially would have preferred to avoid. Many of the welfare advances that Bevin's Ministry of Labour had introduced during the war were uncontroversial and were accepted as part of the post-war settlement of labour conditions. On other industrial questions, however, the consensus was less secure. The Labour party was committed to the nationalisation of public utilities and of the coal industry. These were not part of the Conservative programme, nor were they agreed by the coalition before 1945 in the way that the welfare measures were. A more specific point of controversy was the legal position of the trade unions. Labour had tried without success to persuade Churchill to agree to the repeal of the 1927 Trades Disputes Act. The Conservatives were prepared to recognise the contribution which organised Labour had made to the war. They were not prepared to offer a goodwill concession to the unions as a reward for their support for the government during the war years.

Doubts about the depth of the industrial consensus raise the further question of whether the wartime 'solution' to the Labour question was transferable to the conditions of peacetime. The war years were exceptional in a number of ways: the existence of an external threat which enjoined national unity and forced employers and workers to collaborate for the common cause; the extent of the powers which the state had acquired to direct labour, ban strikes and so on. Even in wartime unity had been difficult to enforce, as the rising number of strikes and industrial disputes had shown. In the face of determined strikers, such as the Betteshanger colliery workers in 1942 or the 200,000 miners of Yorkshire and South Wales in 1944, the law was impotent. With the return of peace the industrial consensus was likely to be more difficult to maintain. Employers and unions alike were eager to resume bargaining unfettered by wartime controls. There was criticism too of the corporatist trend of wartime policies, in which decisions were struck between ministers and national representatives of the unions and employers, and concern about its dangerous political implications. Aneurin Bevan denounced what he called 'the enfranchisement of the corporate society and the disfranchisement of the individual'. He warned his fellow socialists against submitting to 'the corporate rule of Big Business and collaborationist Labour leaders'.[43] As 'normalcy' returned, it was going to be increasingly hard

113

for ministers to contain the tendency to conflict and for 'collaborationist Labour leaders' to maintain command of their rank-and-file. Co-operation between unions and government might be possible, particularly if the government fulfilled its promises of economic prosperity. But the divergent interests of industrial politics were likely to want a wider freedom of manoeuvre than the wartime system allowed.

There is a final political point to be made. The wartime system worked, in part at least, because of the existence after 1940 of a coalition government containing the leaders of all three main political parties. In the spring of 1945 the Labour and Liberal parties decided that they did not wish to prolong the coalition beyond the defeat of Germany. On 23 May 1945, Churchill submitted his resignation as the head of the coalition to the King; he formed a caretaker Conservative administration and normal party politics were resumed, with a general election set to take place in July. Since 1931 both the political and industrial aspects of the Labour question had been, in a sense, in abeyance, first because of the effects of the crisis of 1931 and the depression, then because of the war. Yet the war had greatly strengthened the Labour movement across all sections of the politico-industrial front. Labour ministers had helped to win the war and plan the peace. They were more in tune with the post-Beveridge mood of the nation than were Churchill and his colleagues. The unions, meanwhile, had gained in size, influence and prestige during the course of the war. The political and industrial lines of demarcation were actually sharper in Britain in 1945 than the concept of a transferable wartime consensus allows. If that is so, as the voters went to the polls in July 1945 labour questions were set once more to become a topic of political controversy and the Labour question was about to enter a new phase.

5

BRITISH POLITICS AND THE LABOUR QUESTION SINCE 1945

Two factors kept the Labour question high on the political agenda after 1945. One was the consolidation of the Conservative-Labour two-party system, based loosely (or so it was believed) on the assertion respectively of the industrial perspectives of the employers and the trade unions. The other was Britain's continuing long-term decline as a world economic power, which made industrial policy a central concern of governments of both parties and issues like productivity and wage restraint of prime political importance. The election in 1945 of a majority Labour government committed to a programme of nationalisation and the restoration of trade union immunities seemed to conform to a pattern of party politics derived from industrial conflict, even if the reality was rather different and a fair degree of harmony (political and industrial) persisted through the 1940s and 1950s. When the two-party system began to break up in the 1960s the Liberals attacked a habit of adversarial politics which they said mirrored and exacerbated the antagonism of management and unions. There were those too who sought to place the blame for Britain's economic and industrial problems on an outdatedly confrontational framework of industrial relations and on the unrestrained growth of trade union power. Such criticisms were muted during the Attlee governments of 1945–51 and the thirteen years of Conservative rule which followed, when industrial relations and relations between the government and the unions were mostly good. From the mid-1960s, however, as economic performance faltered and industrial unrest increased, the control, or harnessing, of union power became a standing preoccupation for politicians of all parties, Labour included. Labour's relations with the unions were strained throughout the Wilson and Callaghan years, the 'social contract' of the 1970s notwithstanding. The Conservative party of Edward Heath and Margaret Thatcher attempted to tame the unions by legislative means. In 1974 this led to the downfall of the Heath government, but Mrs Thatcher's return to power in 1979 was the starting point for a more successful programme of trade union reform. In the process, the last vestiges of the post-war consensus were destroyed. With the Labour party in opposition, the unions in disarray and unemployment once again high, it was not immediately clear whether the policies of the 1980s simply marked a temporary return to the conditions of the 1930s, or whether, in the era of 'Thatcherism', the Labour question was, after more than a century, finally losing its place at the heart of political debate.

Corporatism and Consensus, 1945–64

Despite the socialist euphoria which surrounded it, the Labour landslide of 1945 can be interpreted, on one level at least, as a victory for the wartime consensus rather than as a purely partisan triumph. Labour was more closely associated in the minds of the electorate with policies of industrial planning, welfarism and state corporatism than were the Conservatives. The record of coalition Labour ministers like Bevin, Attlee, Dalton and Morrison, the party's long-standing commitment to social equality and its perceived capacity for cooperation with the trade unions, all suggested that Labour was more to be trusted to implement a programme of reconstruction than was a Conservative party supposedly lukewarm in its enthusiasm for the Beveridge proposals and still popularly identified with the depression, unemployment and waste of the inter-war years.[1] Of course, since the parties were competing with one another for votes there was a partisan element to Labour's success, and other factors played their part in determining the outcome of the electoral contest. Churchill, for all his qualities as a war leader (perhaps in some ways because of them), misjudged the mood of the electorate and conducted a largely negative campaign, typified by the 'Gestapo' smear with which he tried to awaken fears of what life under a Labour administration would be like. The Liberals, even with Beveridge as one of their 306 candidates, presented a diminishing challenge and were not capable of forming a government. Labour had better organisation as well as superior leadership and policies with a wider popular appeal. For once, too, it benefited from the working of the electoral system which gave it 393 seats and a majority of 146 over all other parties for only 48 per cent of the popular vote. The Conservatives suffered their worst defeat since 1906, winning only 197 seats, while the Liberals, with a mere twelve MPs, seemed to be on the verge of extinction as a parliamentary force.[2]

Looked at in another way, the Labour governments of 1945–51 were not merely the beneficiaries of a wartime consensus; in their foreign and domestic policies alike they effectively shaped a new consensus for Britain in the post-war world.[3] There was the same sense of purposive reforming energy that had actuated the Liberal ministries of 1906–14, much of it again directed to social or industrial ends. Attlee's first government created the framework of the modern welfare state. A comprehensive scheme of National Insurance was introduced in 1946, complemented by the National Assistance Act of 1948. Aneurin Bevan, the left-wing rebel turned conciliator, was responsible as Minster of Health and housing for establishing the National Health Service and for initiating public house-building programmes to repair some of the ravages of the war years. In industry, nationalisation was the preferred policy for taking industries into 'public ownership'. The nationalisation of the Bank of England in 1946 was followed by that of the coal industry and the railways, canals and road haulage in 1947–8, electricity and gas in 1948–9 and the iron and steel industry in 1951.

The Conservative party had to adapt itself to this leftward, interventionist shift in policy. In fact this was less difficult than might be supposed. There was considerable Conservative support for the Labour government's welfare measures which, while criticised in detail, were not resolutely opposed.[4] Similarly, with the exceptions of the iron and steel industry and road transport, the government's programme of nationalisation was less contentious in practice than it had been in principle. Its motivation was mainly one of improving efficiency, which Conservatives could accept. Labour's nationalisation schemes were confined in the main to run-down, decaying heavy industries in which state control was the most effective way of promoting rationalisation (which had been one of the aims of Conservative policy in the 1930s). Private owners were generously compensated and their capital was freed for productive investment elsewhere. Management structures in the nationalised industries were left in place and the government explicitly ruled out any intention of introducing workers' control. Eighty per cent of industry remained in private hands. It was comparatively easy, therefore, for the Conservatives, in R. A. Butler's *Industrial Charter* of 1947, to accept the measures of nationalisation which had already been carried out as final and to agree that the major public utilities should be run by the state provided that manufacturing industry was left in the private sector. Before the election of 1950 the Conservatives also pledged themselves to maintain the structure of the welfare state, if and when they were returned to power.

The existence of a broad area of cross-party agreement on industrial and welfare policy was a good illustration of the way in which the post-war consensus built upon the shared legacy of wartime cooperation. Another example of the way in which the Attlee government made use of this legacy was provided by its determination to maintain good relations with the trade unions and to involve them (and, for that matter, the employers too) in post-war economic and industrial planning.

This represented a change from earlier Labour governments, when minority administrations had felt obliged to emphasise their independence from the unions for electoral reasons. But the wartime experience had integrated Labour more fully into the machinery of government and won gradual acceptance from all sides of industry for more corporate structures of decision making. In 1945 there was in any case greater unanimity between the political and industrial wings of the Labour movement than there had been in the 1920s. The unions had helped to shape Labour's election programme and they shared the aims of the party's leaders. Bevin, although now Foreign Secretary rather than Minister of Labour, was still a massive presence in the government. One of the first steps taken by the new government was to repeal the Trades Disputes Act of 1927, thereby satisfying a long-standing trade union demand. In the years that followed, the unions were consulted about many of the reforms which the government introduced and about the general lines of economic policy. TUC representatives were appointed to the National Production Advisory Council set up by Stafford Cripps, the President of the Board of Trade, and to other similar bodies. A number of prominent trade union figures such as Walter Citrine and Ebby Edwards of the National Union of Mineworkers (as the MFGB had become in 1944) were made members of the boards of the newly nationalised industries (although giving up trade union office was a condition of appointment). Citrine (who received a knighthood and later a peerage) even became chairman of the British Electricity Authority created as a result of nationalisation in 1948.

In return for their increased influence, the unions naturally had to make some concessions. When the Labour government took office the unions were persuaded to agree to the continuation of wartime procedures for the settlement of industrial disputes, including the retention of Order 1305 and the National Arbitration Tribunal. The implementation of the 1942 Restoration of Pre-War Practices Act was also delayed. Both measures reflected the belief of Bevin, and his successor as Minister of Labour, George Isaacs, in the need for a more controlled approach to industrial relations than that which had been followed after 1918. The other crucial factor in their minds was the level of wage settlements, particularly in the light of the severity of Britain's post-war economic problems of indebtedness and a weakening pound. As has been seen, wages had not been subject to statutory limits during the war, although the government had urged moderation on union negotiators. This was even more necessary after 1945, in order to prevent inflation and to boost the competitiveness of British exports, the flow of which had virtually dried up during the war but which were now vital to the country's economic recovery. In response to pressure from ministers, TUC leaders agreed to enforce a policy of wage restraint as their contribution to the government's overall economic strategy. Such self-denial on the part of the unions more than justified the policy of co-operation as far as the politicians were concerned. Throughout the late 1940s industrial stoppages ran at about or only slightly above their wartime levels. Although the period was one of more or less full employment (unemployment touched a 'peak' of 3.1 per cent in 1947 compared with an average of ten per cent in the 1930s) wage inflation was kept within acceptable bounds. An effective partnership between government and unions was shown as being integral to the task of successful economic management.

As in the war, however, the quasi-corporatist consensus had its limits. Government and unions shared a common interest in the health of the economy but their perspectives and priorities were necessarily different. Agreement between ministers and TUC leaders did not automatically satisfy or placate the union rank-and-file. Indeed, sometimes it had the reverse effect. For example, whereas the union leadership endorsed the government's nationalisation programme, there was strong criticism from some sections of trade union opinion of the failure to provide for genuine workers' control. Indignation was increased when leading figures from the trade union movement retired from their union positions to take up lucrative posts on the boards of nationalised industries. There was resentment too at the continuation of 'no strike' provisions and wage restraint. A number of stoppages took place in defiance of the strike ban, for instance in the docks in 1948 and 1949, forcing the government to invoke Emergency Powers legislation and to mobilise troops to break the strikes and maintain supplies.[5] In 1950, against the advice of the General Council, the TUC voted to abandon the wage restraint policy, thereby breaking its compact with a Labour government already buffeted by the successive financial crises of 1947 and 1949, by fears of inflation and by continuing balance of payments problems. Underneath these very public manifestations of discontent lay the further threat of Communist infiltration of the Labour movement. Some major unions such as the AEU and the Electrical Trades Union were either under Communist control or had strong Communist minorities among their officers. The TGWU was so alarmed by the spread of Communist influence that in 1949 its general secretary, Arthur Deakin, persuaded the union conference to ban known Communists from holding any office.[6]

Under attack from its erstwhile allies in the unions, by 1949–50 the Labour government was facing a renewed challenge from the Conservative opposition. Although the Conservatives had accepted the main features of Labour's domestic programme, they were critical of the slowness with which the government was dismantling wartime controls and lifting rationing, as well as what they considered to be the more fundamental shortcomings of its economic policy.[7] A major issue at the 1950 election was the government's proposal to nationalise the iron and steel industry. Industrialists and businessmen had mounted an effective propaganda campaign against this measure, which the Conservatives opposed and about which even some Labour ministers were having second thoughts. How significant this was in deciding the outcome of the 1950 election it is hard to say. Labour actually increased its total vote from 11.9 million in 1945 to 13.2 million in 1950 (although this represented a slight fall in its national percentage share), but the Conservatives also received an extra two million votes and increased their total of seats from 197 to 282, reducing Labour's majority to five. This was enough to maintain the government in power and to enable it to force through its nationalisation of iron and steel. But the strain on a tired and ageing Labour leadership of sustaining their position in these difficult circumstances soon told. Following the resignation of Bevan and two of his colleagues over the size of the rearmament programme and the imposition of health charges, in October 1951 Attlee decided on a further appeal to the country. Labour again increased its vote for a diminishing return, its number of seats falling from 315 to 295. The main reason for this was the reduced presence of the Liberals, who fielded only 109 candidates in 1951 compared with 475 in 1950 and whose vote slumped accordingly to just 730,546. The Conservatives were the principal beneficiaries, and with their allies the National Liberals won enough seats (321) to give them a narrow overall majority. Churchill replaced Attlee as Prime Minister and formed his first (and only) peacetime government.[8]

The Churchill government carried out the denationalisation of the iron and steel industry and partially returned the road haulage industry to private ownership. Its industrial policies were otherwise in line with the *Industrial Charter* of 1947. The Minister of Labour, Walter Monckton, continued the corporatist strategy of consultation with unions and employers, to the extent that the unions even agreed to appoint representatives to the supervisory board for iron and steel denationalisation. Macmillan, the Minister of Housing, continued Bevan's work of the 1940s, fulfilling an election pledge to build 300,000 new houses a year. R. A. Butler as Chancellor of the Exchequer followed policies sufficiently similar to those of his Labour predecessor, Hugh Gaitskell, for *The Economist* in 1954 to invent the figure of 'Mr Butskell' as the supposed embodiment of consensus politics. In general, industrial relations remained quiet; full employment, the end of rationing and a slow rise in wages produced feelings of affluence and wellbeing. This is not to say that there were no labour problems. Monckton had to intervene in 1953–4 to prevent damaging national strikes on the railways and in the engineering and shipbuilding industries. The withdrawal of Order 1305 by the previous Labour government in August 1951 removed legal sanctions for use against strikers and the unions reacted coolly to suggestions for permanent arbitration machinery to be operated by the Ministry of Labour. Nor did they become any more amenable to ideas of wage restraint. Already there were indications that as the emergency atmosphere of wartime receded, and as a new generation of trade union leaders emerged to take over from those who had operated the machinery of wartime co-operation, the task of securing trade union endorsement for government policy was likely to increase in difficulty.

These signs were there to be read in the later years of Conservative rule. This did not stop the Conservative party from strengthening its hold on power. Anthony Eden succeeded Churchill as Prime Minister on the latter's retirement in 1955 and the Conservatives were rewarded with an increased majority at the election which Eden called to secure a personal mandate. Despite the traumas of the Suez crisis and Eden's enforced resignation, Harold Macmillan as the new Prime Minister was able to win a third term with an even larger majority for the Conservatives in 1959. But there were problems ahead. Levels of industrial unrest were increasing even before Macmillan's succession to office. Unemployment was still low, the 'stop go' policies of Conservative Chancellors in the 1950s had resulted in a steady rise in wage inflation. The dramatic announcement by the Chancellor, Selwyn Lloyd, of a 'pay pause' in the summer of 1961 as part of an emergency package of economic measures signalled the extent to which the government was losing control of the economy. It also gratuitously inflamed relations with the trade unions, who had not been consulted beforehand. The TUC did agree to co-operate in the setting up of the National Economic Development Council on which they would meet with employers and ministers to discuss issues of economic policy, but they refused to have any further policies of wage restraint imposed on them or to take part in the deliberations of the National Incomes Commission which was established in 1962. The common endeavours of 1945–50 had, by the early 1960s, become a potentially much more antagonistic relationship.

The cooling off in relations between government and unions may have reflected adversely on the managerial skills of Conservative governments in the post-Churchill era. Even so, through the 1950s at least, growing union unrest probably worked in the Conservatives' favour from an electoral point of view. A series of inter-union demarcation disputes in the docks, the newspaper industry and on the railways in 1954–5 tarnished the public image of the trade unions and possibly affected the level of support for the Labour party at the 1955 election. Conservative publicists made great play with the role of the unions in Labour party policy making, capitalising on mounting public hostility to the unions to damage Labour's electoral chances.[9] The events of the 1950s certainly provided plenty of ammunition for this line of attack. For most of the decade after 1951 the Labour party was riven by internal conflict between left and right in which the unions played an active part.[10] In the early 1950s the unions mostly supported the policies of the party leadership against the Bevanite left. From the mid-1950s, however, some of the major unions (including the TGWU under its new general secretary, Frank Cousins) shifted their ground. The climax of this swing to the left came at the party conference at Scarborough in 1960, where the block votes of the TGWU, AEU, railwaymen and shop workers were instrumental in securing a majority for the policy of unilateral nuclear disarmament against the wishes of the party's leader, Hugh Gaitskell (who had defeated Bevan and Morrison for the succession to Attlee in 1955). The vote was reversed the following year, but most of the damage had already been done. The old claim of the other parties that a Labour government meant a trade union government was given an added twist by the new fear that a trade union government would be a government committed to increasingly left-wing policies, abrogating the 1950s consensus in domestic and foreign affairs.

Fears of the consequences of electing a union-dominated Labour party helped to generate a Liberal revival as the Conservative government of Harold Macmillan ran into trouble in 1962–3. The Liberal victory in the Orpington by-election of 1962 encouraged speculation on the part of the Liberal leader

Jo Grimond about a 'realignment' of the left to produce a mod-
ernised version of the pre-1914 progressive alliance. Such talk,
as so often in Liberal history, proved premature. At the general
election of 1964 the Liberals polled over three million votes
but won only nine seats. Labour, led by Harold Wilson in place
of Hugh Gaitskell (who had died in 1963),[11] benefited from
the Liberal upsurge which was mainly at the Conservatives'
expense. Although polling fewer votes than in 1959, the party
did much better than in the previous election in terms of seats,
winning 317 as opposed to 258. The wounds inflicted by the
Bevan-Gaitskell struggles of the 1950s had almost healed; union
leaders did all they could to avoid embarrassing the party at the
polls. With Harold Wilson talking the language of industrial
modernisation and technological revolution, Labour returned
somewhat shakily to power with a majority of four, consigning
Alec Douglas-Home's Conservatives to the opposition benches
for the first time since 1951. The victory of 1964 lacked the
sweeping endorsement of 1945, but it was no less welcome for
that. Whether it could be turned into more than a temporary
interlude between Conservative governments depended to a
large extent on how successful the Wilson cabinet was in solving
the problems of British industry. Could the close relations
between politicians and unions which had helped the Attlee
government to weather the storms of the 1940s be revived
to provide the basis for a more stable, planned approach to
economic activity than the Conservative administrations of the
1950s had been able to deliver?

'In Place of Strife', 1964–79

In the 1960s and 1970s the 'Labour question' in all its facets re-
emerged with a force it had not shown for a generation. There
was renewed debate about labour conditions – issues such as
the terms of employment, equal pay for women – and about
industrial and economic policy, as post-war hopes of limitless
prosperity began to be eroded by rising unemployment, high
inflation and low rates of growth. The questions of industrial

relations and trade union law were brought to the fore by the growing incidence of unofficial strikes and the reluctance of the unions to co-operate in policies of wage restraint. Whereas in the 1950s foreign observers had looked with approbation on the comparatively harmonious character of labour relations in Britain, by the late 1960s there was talk of the 'British disease' of endemic workplace conflict. Their failure to come to terms with 'trade union power' contributed substantially to the fall of two, possibly three, of the governments which held office in these years. The inability of the Labour party in particular to work effectively with the trade unions raised doubts about its capacity to function at all as a governing party in an industrial society, fuelling the search for alternatives and reopening the party-political aspects of the Labour question.

Some of these trends were apparent before the 1964 election and concern about them was reflected in the narrow margin of Labour's victory. Labour greatly improved its position at the election of 1966, winning 363 seats to the Conservatives' 253 and gaining an overall majority of 98, a result so far without parallel other than in the exceptional circumstances of 1945.[12] But the taste of victory was evanescent. A long sequence of by-election and local election defeats soon set in. A record of progressive social reforms was more than outweighed by disappointments on the economic and industrial front. In this respect, the Wilson governments of 1964–70 faced a situation that was not wholly dissimilar to that which had confronted the Attlee governments after 1945.[13] They inherited a serious balance of payments deficit; mounting pressure on sterling led to a devaluation of the pound in 1967. The government's attempt to manage the economy through a Department of Economic Affairs and a 'National Plan' was pushed off course, just as the planning initiatives of the earlier Labour government had been. There were echoes of previous policies – the renationalisation of the steel industry was one – but no new ideas. Unemployment increased from 380,000 in 1964 to 570,000 in 1970; the number of industrial disputes per year rose from 2,524 to 3,906 in the same period (10.9 million days lost rather than 2.2 million). A wage-price inflationary spiral was at work well before the government left office.

The issue of pay was one of the most intractable with which the government had to deal. As has been seen, both the Attlee governments of 1945–51 and the Conservative governments of the 1950s had attempted to persuade the unions to agree to a voluntary policy of restraint, ultimately without success. Control over pay was something which the Wilson government also sought to achieve. In a 'Declaration of Intent' on productivity, prices and incomes in December 1964 the government set a 3–3½ per cent norm for pay increases, based on the assumption of four per cent per annum economic growth. A Prices and Incomes Board was appointed to monitor increases, though the norms had no legal force. After the 1966 election, with a more secure parliamentary majority and the pressure of an impending sterling crisis (aggravated by a national seamen's strike in May-July), the government announced a formal pay freeze to operate for six months, followed by a further six months of 'severe restraint'. All increases had by law to be notified to the Prices and Incomes Board. These measures provoked considerable disquiet in the trade unions. Frank Cousins, the TGWU general secretary who had joined Wilson's cabinet in 1964 as Minister for Technology, resigned from the government. Unions like the TGWU and the AUEW opposed the government policy at the TUC conference in September. The resulting 'pay pause' was largely ineffective, merely delaying the implementation of inflationary settlements and storing up material for a subsequent wages 'explosion'.[14]

Difficulties over pay inevitably placed a strain on relations between the government and the TUC and made it harder to find ways of reducing industrial unrest. Some measures were introduced on the basis of agreement between government and unions. The Trade Disputes Act of 1965 closed a legal loophole in the 1906 Act recently revealed by the case of Rookes v Barnard.[15] The TUC welcomed measures such as the Redundancy Pay Act of 1965 and the Equal Pay Act of 1970. More contentious, at least in prospect, was the cabinet's decision to appoint the Donovan Commission on

Trade Unions and Employers' Associations in 1965. This was the most searching enquiry into industrial relations since the Royal Commissions of 1891–4 and 1902–5, possibly even since that of 1867–9. Its brief was to investigate the causes of the breakdown in industrial relations that was occurring in the 1960s and to make recommendations for government action.[16] Its report, issued in 1968, provided a detailed insight into what its authors described as the 'two systems' of industrial relations in Britain, a 'formal system' embodied in official institutions and an informal system, 'created by the actual behaviour of trade unions and employers' associations, of managers, shop stewards and workers'.[17] This was a crucial distinction. It was also one which implicitly warned about the limits of government action, since the 'informal system' was largely beyond the control of national trade union leaders, placing power in the hands of local negotiators and shop stewards whose actions contributed to the rising tide of unofficial and localised plant-based strikes in the car industry and elsewhere.

In the sense that Donovan was basically a blueprint for inaction, it contained nothing to which the TUC could object, even if it suggested the increasing irrelevance of national leaders in pay bargaining.[18] Significantly, George Woodcock, the TUC general secretary, was one of the members of the Donovan Commission and did not dissent from the final report. For the Wilson government, however, the Donovan report did not go far enough. They speedily implemented its main recommendation, the setting up of an Industrial Relations Commission, with George Woodcock as chairman, but they determined to go further in trying to provide a legal framework which would rein in the tendency to engage in unofficial strikes.[19] In January 1969, Barbara Castle, who had succeeded the trade unionist Ray Gunter at the Ministry of Labour in April 1968 to become the first Secretary of State for Employment and Productivity, published her controversial White Paper, *In Place of Strife*.[20] This was not in any way intended as an 'anti-union' document. Indeed, Castle described it as a 'charter' for labour, in that it guaranteed the right to join a trade union, provided assistance for unions wishing to amalgamate and protection for workers in the event of unfair dismissal. Yet what attracted most attention was not this aspect of the proposed reforms, nor the promise to compel employers to grant recognition to trade unions. Much greater emphasis was placed on the additional powers which the government intended to take to enable it to intervene more directly in the conduct of industrial relations. The idea of a 'conciliation pause' was mooted which would allow a threatened strike to be suspended while efforts were made to find a peaceful settlement. The Secretary of State was to be given ultimate power to resolve inter-union disputes where the unions themselves proved unable to do so. The government was also to be able to require strike ballots to be held before industrial action could take place.

Despite what in retrospect may seem moderate, even sensible, proposals, *In Place of Strife* caused a storm in the Labour movement. In a Commons debate on the White Paper in March, 53 Labour MPs voted against the government and a further 40 abstained. Party whips predicted worse revolts if the government pressed ahead with legislation, while even some members of the cabinet, notably James Callaghan, declared themselves against the plan. The TUC, meanwhile, was implacably hostile to the idea of legal interference in its internal affairs, with the TGWU and the AUEW again in the van of opposition to the government. Eventually a compromise of sorts was reached, although one which was in effect a humiliating rebuff for Castle and Wilson at the hands of their opponents. The Industrial Relations Bill based on the White Paper was withdrawn, and in its place the TUC adopted a 'Programme for Action', which included a 'solemn and binding' undertaking that the General Council would use its influence to reduce the incidence of wildcat strikes. The unions had succeeded in preserving the voluntary system of bargaining against government intervention, even if, as it turned out, only temporarily. In the process, they had severely damaged the reputation of the Labour government and may even had contributed to its defeat at the hands of the Conservatives in the election of June 1970.

The members of the incoming Heath government had apparently learned nothing from the events of 1969, nor do they seem fully to have absorbed the lessons of the Donovan Commission. In 1968 the Conservative party had adopted its own proposals for trade union reform under the title of a *Fair Deal at Work*. These were similar to the plans which Labour had abandoned and they formed the basis of the 1971 Industrial Relations Act introduced by Heath's Employment Secretary, Robert Carr.[21] The main institutional innovation of the Act was to set up a National Industrial Relations Court, under the presidency of Sir John Donaldson. The court had the power to impose a 'cooling off' period before strikes took place and to require the holding of strike ballots. It went beyond the previous Labour proposals by introducing fines for unions found guilty of 'unfair practices'; by making collective agreements legally binding; and by amending the rules governing the operations of 'closed shop' arrangements. A final provision required unions to register with the Registrar of Trade Unions and Employers' Associations if they wished to retain legal protection under existing trade union law. The Registrar was given the power to compel unions to change their rules where these did not comply with the terms of the new Act.

The measure met a predictable furore of opposition from the unions. The TUC campaigned against the Bill and when it became law in August 1971 pledged itself to work for its repeal.[22] What amounted to a sustained programme of civil disobedience was instituted. The unions refused to recognise the jurisdiction of the NIRC and the TUC instructed member unions not to register their activities or, if they were already registered, to de-register immediately. Most unions complied with the instruction; those which did not were suspended from the TUC the following year. The NIRC attempted to assert its authority, but to no avail. The TGWU and AUEW were both fined for contempt for failing to answer the summons of the court; the engineers had some of their assets sequestrated. But the impotence of the court in the face of resolute union hostility was demonstrated by two disputes in 1972. In April the court imposed a cooling off period and a strike ballot on the National Union of Railwaymen, only to find that in the subsequent vote the railwaymen declared by a margin of 6–1 in favour of a strike. Then, in July, the so-called 'Pentonville five' were jailed for picketing the Midland Cold Storage Depot in London as part of an extension of a dispute in the docks. Their incarceration triggered a national dock strike which only the intervention of the obscure figure of the 'Official Solicitor' and his order for the men's release brought to an end.

These instances were enough to show the unworkability of the Act and its uselessness as a tool for improving industrial relations, something which the employers, if not the government, were quick to recognise. However, union discontent over the government's legal reforms was conflated with the wider struggle over pay, and it was this which led to the most serious industrial confrontations. The Heath government had initially abandoned attempts to enforce a policy of wage restraint. The Prices and Incomes Board established by the previous Labour government had been abolished. But with the level of wage settlements running at well over ten per cent by early 1972 a more stringent counter-inflation policy was seen to be necessary. A 'standstill' on prices and wages was accordingly introduced, followed in 1973 by Stages II and III of a strategy intended to limit the total annual growth of the nation's wage bill to no more than seven per cent. These measures were probably too far removed from the realities of the situation to have worked very well under any circumstances, but they were finally undermined by two powerful factors. One was the additional inflationary pressure produced by the sharp increase in oil prices which followed the war in the Middle East in 1973. The other, nearer to home, was the continuing opposition of the trade unions, already antagonised by the Industrial Relations Act, to any form of wage control.

Although many different groups of workers in both the public and private sectors were involved in the wage battles of 1972–3, it was the miners who had the greatest political impact. In January 1972 the NUM rejected the Coal Board's offer of an eight per cent rise and launched an all-out national strike. The strike was sustained by an aggressive campaign of mass picketing (organised by, among others, Arthur Scargill of the Yorkshire miners), which helped to mobilise the support of other unions for the miners' cause. Scargill's blockade of the Saltley Coke Depot, and the use of similar tactics by squads of 'flying pickets' elsewhere, prevented the movement of coal to the power stations and brought the economy almost to a standstill, forcing the government to introduce a three-day working week and leading to widespread power cuts.[23] The miners won their increase (worth as much as 24 per cent in some cases) and the government's pay policy was in tatters. More than that, the NUM were encouraged to repeat their tactics in the following year, imposing an overtime ban late in 1973 and voting in a ballot in January 1974 for a strike to begin in February if their new wage claims were not met. Stung into action by the prospect of having to capitulate a second time to the miners, the government reimposed the three-day week and introduced a range of restrictions to conserve fuel, including a 50 mph speed limit and reducing television transmission times. TUC leaders and others offered possible compromises to end the dispute but the government preferred instead the ultimate sanction of a general election, Prime Minister Edward Heath hoping that the electorate would give him a clear mandate for upholding the authority of parliamentary government against what he saw as the dangerous sectionalism inherent in the exercise of trade union power.

The general election of February 1974 seemed to provide a perfect illustration of the consequences of the twentieth-century industrialisation of party politics. The Conservatives, with their slogan of 'Firm Action for a Fair Britain', ran a frankly anti-union campaign, stressing the irresponsibility of the unions and defending, as best they could, their own record of economic management. Labour promised that it would 'Get Britain Back to Work' by settling the miners' dispute and working with the trade unions on the basis of a 'social contract' drawn up by the TUC-Labour party liaison committee which had been set up in 1972 to heal the divisions created by *In Place of Strife*.[24] Perhaps the most significant factor of the election, though, was the strong Liberal revival. Under their popular leader, Jeremy Thorpe, the Liberals promised industrial conciliation and co-partnership, an end to the two-party capital-labour dogfight and a new era of consensual politics. Their total of six million votes was the highest ever polled by the Liberal party in a general election, even though it brought them only a derisory 14 seats. Labour emerged as the largest single party but with no overall majority. On this unsteady basis, Harold Wilson formed a minority Labour government.[25]

The early actions of the Wilson government appeared to conform to the capital-labour dichotomy of parties. The government settled the miners' strike by the simple expedient of conceding virtually all of the union's demands, amounting to a pay rise in the order of 29 per cent, thereby fuelling a further inflationary spiral as other unions sought to make this the 'going rate' for their members in the annual pay round. Michael Foot, the former Bevanite who took over as Secretary of State for Employment, repealed the 1971 Industrial Relations Act and introduced an Employment Protection Act favourable to the unions. He also promised a return to free collective bargaining and the consequent abandonment of the previous government's counter-inflation strategy. The 'union-friendly' Advisory, Conciliation and Arbitration Service replaced the cumbersome, legalistic machinery of the National Industrial Relations Court.

Yet, as in the 1920s, the simple capital-labour categorisation of parties breaks down upon a closer examination. For one thing, the employers' organisation, the CBI, had not supported the Conservative Industrial Relations Act, and their director, Campbell Adamson, was openly critical of the Conservatives during the election campaign.[26] The other principal limitation of the 'industrial party' model is that it does not adequately take account of the Labour party's equivocal relationship with the trade unions, especially when in government. The controversy over *In Place of Strife* had shown the kind of tensions that existed. These were relaxed in opposition in 1970–74, when Labour politicians comfortably denounced the Conservatives' industrial relations policy and negotiated the 'social contract' with trade union leaders. But as soon as

Labour returned to office the old problems re-emerged. The 1974–5 wages round, according to one commentator, was 'an unmitigated disaster'.[27] Wage increases of twenty per cent or more for groups like the miners produced soaring inflation and growing discontent among low-paid public sector workers who could not command such huge settlements. Unemployment was rising at an alarming rate and topped the one million mark in October 1975. By the middle of 1976 a renewed sterling crisis had precipitated the intervention of the International Monetary Fund and compelled the Chancellor, Denis Healey, to introduce a deflationary package of public spending cuts. As the economy careered out of control measures to limit pay and subdue industrial unrest again took on an overriding importance.

At first the unions were more co-operative than they had been in the past. Largely under the influence of Jack Jones, the general secretary of the TGWU and one of the authors – along with the TUC general secretary, Len Murray, and Hugh Scanlon of the AUEW – of the 'social contract', the TUC agreed to apply a voluntary policy of wage restraint, setting a flat rate target of £6 per week as the norm for increases in 1975. In 1976 this was replaced by a more flexible £2.50–£4.00 range, although in practice the higher figure became the norm. The aim was to pursue a policy which would be fair to those on low pay, even at the expense of squeezing the differentials of higher-paid workers. The policy had some effect, but it was at best a short-term expedient and could not be expected to hold. In 1977 the TUC voted for an orderly return to 'unfettered' collective bargaining and an end to pay restraint. The unions were also unhappy with the proposals of the Bullock Committee on Industrial Democracy, which they feared would, if imple-mented, reduce their freedom of action by tying them in to management structures, with trade union representatives being present in the boardroom and party to management decisions. The suspicion with which this idea was greeted, as well as the engrained opposition to pay policy, emphasises the extreme reluctance with which union leaders entered into corporate relationships with government and employers and offers a glimpse of the highly developed individualist tendencies which were bound in the end to undermine the kind of co-operation between unions and the state which had been part of the wartime consensus.[28] In the context of the late 1970s, this suggested that there were further confrontations ahead.

The Labour government's political position remained far from strong. The narrow majority which it had gained in the October 1974 election had evaporated by early 1977 and the government was forced to negotiate a pact with the Liberals to avoid the loss of a parliamentary vote of confidence. The replacement of Harold Wilson as Prime Minister by James Callaghan on the former's retirement in 1976 had done nothing to improve the party's fortunes, which were depressed even more by divisions over government proposals for Scottish and Welsh devolution and by continuing industrial troubles, notably the violence on the picket lines outside the Grunwick laboratories in London in 1978. Callaghan made matters worse for himself by ruling out an election in the autumn of 1978. The Lib-Lab pact had come to an end in July; a 10 per cent pay rise guideline had held the inflation line in 1977–8, but no more; and the assembled delegates at the TUC were surprised to be told, through the mischievous medium of a music hall song, that the expected election was to be delayed until the spring or summer of 1979. This proved to be a mistake. A five per cent pay guideline for 1978–9 was far too rigid and there were widespread protest strikes by public sector workers and others during what became known as the 'winter of discontent'.[29] Yet again a Labour government was seen to be at loggerheads with those who were supposed to be its natural supporters, the trade unions. Inflation resumed its inexorable rise and the government's economic policy was largely discredited, despite some earlier signs of recovery. In March 1979 there was another setback when the devolution proposals failed to gain the necessary majorities in referenda in Scotland and Wales. On 28 March the government was beaten by a single vote on a motion of no confidence moved by the leader of the Opposition, Margaret Thatcher. At the ensuing general election in May, Labour stumbled to defeat, the Liberal revival of 1974 was checked and the Conservatives returned to power, having won the chance to atone for the ignominious failures of their previous term of office. Once more the Labour question had played its part in bringing about the downfall of a Labour government and shaping the policies of its successor.

The Thatcher Years, 1979–90

The election of a Conservative government under Margaret Thatcher in 1979 marked a decisive break with the post-war consensus and the return to a more individualist approach to economic and industrial policy. The ideas of 'Thatcherism' were not wholly new: they had affinities with the economic liberalism of the nineteenth century; they had been foreshadowed in the writings of Frederick von Hayek, beginning with his *Road to Serfdom*, published in 1944; and they drew heavily upon the business practice of the United States and the views of Milton Friedman and other economists of the 'monetarist' school. Thatcherism did not even represent a new strand of Conservatism, since Edward Heath had come to power in 1970 committed to a similar brand of free-market theory.[30] But, in the eyes of the Thatcherites, the Heath administration had reneged on its ideals. It had intervened to save troubled industries like Rolls Royce and Upper Clyde Shipbuilders. It had increased public spending and permitted an inflationary expansion of the money supply. Above all, it had failed to overcome the problem of trade union power. When Mrs Thatcher succeeded Edward Heath as Conservative leader in 1975 she was determined that history should not repeat itself. With her collaborators in the Centre for Policy Studies, notably Sir Keith Joseph, she was convinced of the need to reverse the trend towards state corporatism and to challenge the Keynesian assumptions which had hitherto governed post-war economic thinking. Her libertarian, anti-collectivist, anti-union rhetoric appealed alike to those who had been alienated by the excesses of the 'winter of discontent' and to those, including many trade unionists, for whom free market ideas offered an escape from the constraints of pay policy, high taxation and the damaging effects of the inflationary spiral.

One of the most obvious manifestations of the Thatcherite new broom was to be found in the government's programme of trade union reform. Mrs Thatcher's first Employment Secretary, James Prior,[31] persuaded the Prime Minister that this was a sensitive subject best tackled by piecemeal, step-by-step change rather than by a single legislative onslaught. The result was a series of measures which, together, effected many of the alterations in law and practice which had been proposed or introduced by earlier governments, only to be abandoned because of trade union opposition. The process of reform began with two Employment Acts in 1980 and 1982, which gave employers redress against secondary picketing, placed restrictions on the operation of the closed shop and made unions liable for damages if they took unlawful strike action. In 1984, the Trade Union Act made pre-strike ballots compulsory and required that trade union officials should stand for re-election at least once every five years. Two further Employment Acts in 1988 and 1990 made secret ballots compulsory for all union elections, imposed legal liability on unions for unofficial strikes called without a ballot and gave individual union members greater rights of redress against unfair treatment by their own unions. The right not to join a trade union was guaranteed by law. Future measures were contemplated which would revive the idea of making all collective agreements legally binding, re-introduce the 'cooling off' period in industrial disputes and give employees the right to join the union of their choice, regardless of existing inter-union agreements.[32]

The trade union reforms had both a political and an economic purpose. Politically they were intended to demonstrate the government's commitment to dealing with the problem of union power and breaking the cycle of unrest which had disfigured industrial relations in the 1970s. From an economic point of view, the reforms were designed to promote greater flexibility in the labour market and to facilitate the introduction of new working practices which would improve productivity. As such, they were seen as a contribution to the restructuring of British industry and as part of a wider application of free market principles to labour policy. This philosophy was to embrace pay as well as other aspects of the Labour question. Although the incoming Thatcher government in 1979 had made promises during the election to honour awards made by the Clegg Commission on public sector pay, the whole thrust of Conservative policy (as outlined in their manifesto and in the 1977 document, *The Right Approach to the Economy*) was to remove government influence from pay bargaining. Public sector pay would be controlled to some extent by the application of cash limits, and there was to be a general restriction of the money supply to prevent inflation, but the idea of a statutory pay policy was rejected, while nationally agreed norms were regarded as ineffective and conceding too much influence to the unions in determining economic policy. Indeed, not only did the government reject the idea of a pay policy; in due course they also repealed many existing provisions affecting wage rates, allowing wages to 'find their own level' according to market conditions. The abolition of Wages Councils, some of them dating back to Bevin's Act of 1945 or the Liberal Trade Boards Act of 1909, was one instance of this return to a modified form of the mid-Victorian wage fund theory.

Underlying this retreat from direct intervention in the labour market was the abandonment of full employment as a deliberate objective of government policy. Throughout the 1950s and 1960s, Conservative as well as Labour governments had upheld the aim of the 1944 White Paper, easily in the 1950s, less so in the 1960s. Memories of the Thirties cast a long shadow on both sides of the political divide. In the 1970s, however, the first breach in the dyke had been made, as the Wilson and Callaghan governments were unable to prevent unemployment reaching 1¼ million by the time they left office. For the Thatcher government, the reduction of inflation, not of unemployment, was the first priority. While inflation was brought, albeit temporarily, under control in the early and mid-1980s, unemployment was allowed to rise unchecked, exceeding three million by 1983, despite an alteration by the Department of Employment of the basis on which the figures were calculated. This is not to say that high unemployment was used callously as a means of checking inflation, or that ministers were not genuinely concerned about its social and political implications. Some job creation and training measures were introduced.[33] It was argued that trade union reforms and the removal of wage controls would boost employment in the longer term, even if in the short term the reduction of overmanning caused the dole queues to lengthen. But the view that it was no longer within the responsibility, or even the capacity, of the state to maintain employment by Keynesian-type public spending and economic management was a singular shift away from the consensus which had hitherto pertained since the end of the Second World War.

In its second term of office, from 1983 to 1987, the Thatcher government turned its back on the post-war consensus in another respect too. Since the late 1940s, the idea of a 'mixed' economy had been accepted by both of the major parties. The Churchill government of 1951–5 had denationalised steel and road transport, but the other nationalisation measures of the 1945 Labour Government were left intact. As has been noted, later Conservative governments, including the Heath ministry of which Mrs Thatcher was a member, had actually extended the boundaries of state ownership and had invested public funds in industrial development. After 1979 this trend was reversed as part of an ambitious attempt to 'roll back' the frontiers of the state. 'Privatisation' became a central plank of government policy. The sale of public utilities like gas, water, electricity, and of corporations like British Telecom, in addition to the disposal of other assets acquired in the 1960s and 1970s, raised large sums of money for the Treasury and helped to finance reductions in the level of direct personal taxation. It was hoped that it would do even more: that the encouragement of individual share ownership would create a nation of 'consumer capitalists' in the same way that the sale of council houses and the availability of cheap mortgages was creating a nation of property owners. The end of restrictive monopolies (whether of state corporations or trade unions), the restoration of incentives and the virtues of competition were all lauded as components of a more diversified, less dependent, enterprise culture.

Whether or not such a cultural transformation occurred in the 1980s, restructuring on this scale was not a painless process. Levels of labour unrest remained high for much of the Thatcher decade, and although ministers sought to distance themselves from the conflicts that took place, and to deny responsibility for them, the government was nevertheless deeply implicated and its public reputation was affected by the course which disputes took. Some disputes were in any case the direct result of government action, and were in essence political, as for instance the ministerial decision to ban trade unions at the secret GCHQ establishment at Cheltenham. On other occasions trouble arose from the determination of private employers to take a harder line against the unions, their resolve stiffened by the messages emanating from ministerial speeches. The dispute between News International and the printworkers which led to mass picketing of the Wapping plant in protest against redundancies caused by the introduction of new technology was perhaps the best example. The government's main problems, though, were in the nationalised industries and the public sector. In 1980 a lengthy strike in the steel industry forced the management to concede a 16 per cent wage rise. In 1981 there were strikes among civil servants unhappy with the government's pay offer. As spending cuts and cash limits in the public services began to bite there were long-running disputes involving previously non-militant workers such as nurses and hospital staff, ambulancemen and teachers. All of these were dwarfed, however, by the miners' strike of 1984–5, which turned into a fierce clash of wills between the NUM, led by Arthur Scargill, and the Thatcher government.[34] Mrs Thatcher, flushed by her victory over General Galtieri in the Falklands War and bolstered by a second general election victory in 1983, attacked Scargill's miners as 'the enemy within', with whom no compromise was possible. Violence flared repeatedly on the picket lines as the police were mobilised to enable non-strikers to get to work and to prevent the miners from halting the movement of coal as they had in 1972. For a time labour conflict threatened to tear the country apart and to destroy the credibility of the government, in a return to the bad old days of Heathite Britain or an even earlier era of 'collective bargaining by riot'.[35]

Yet this did not happen. Some groups of workers were certainly alienated, either temporarily or permanently, by the government's intransigence or indifference. But gradually their opposition or their will to resist was eroded. The government benefited at times from the tactical errors of their opponents. The miners' strike of 1984–5 was misconceived from the outset. Scargill did not hold a strike ballot and could not rely on 100 per cent support from his members, as was shown when the Nottingham miners broke away from the NUM to form their own Union of Democratic Mineworkers. There was only limited sympathetic action by other unions and the Labour party maintained an embarrassed distance from the dispute. The very aim of the strike – to preserve jobs and pits in a declining industry – was one which was very unlikely to be achieved through strike action. Even so, these factors, important though they were, pale into comparative insignificance against the firm resolve of the Prime Minister and her allies. As early as 1978, one of Mrs Thatcher's closest supporters, Nicholas Ridley, had devised a plan for taking on and defeating the miners as part of a strategy for curbing the power of the trade unions to resist economic change. In the early 1980s coal stocks were built up and strike-proof transport arrangements put in place. A nationally co-ordinated police response network was created to deal with the kind of 'flying pickets' used in the 1972 strike. The government also appointed the hard-line Ian MacGregor as chairman of the NCB, confident that he would stand up to Scargill's militant tactics. MacGregor it was who, in an earlier incarnation as chairman of British Steel, had reacted to the 'defeat' over the pay settlement in 1980 by more than halving the workforce, from 166,000 to 70,000, in the space of three years and preparing the way for the industry's re-privatisation.

After a year-long strike, the miners returned to work to face the continued contraction of their industry and a fresh phase of pit closures. Despite varying levels of support from public opinion, other employees in the health and education services were similarly unsuccessful in their challenge to their public sector employers and the government ministers behind them. Pay increases were won, but the new working practices, productivity norms and other contractual accompaniments of the enterprise-efficiency culture were rigorously enforced throughout the public and private sectors. While the restructuring of the workplace was going on, there were times when the trade union movement seemed to be becoming more and more marginalised. TUC leaders were no longer consulted by government over national policy in the 1980s as they had been in the 1970s; some of Mrs Thatcher's ministers, not to mention the Prime Minister herself, gave the impression of holding the unions in open contempt.

For the unions themselves, the 1980s were a decade of retrenchment and redefinition. The changing composition of the movement which had been under way since the 1960s continued, as membership of old industrial unions like the miners or the steelworkers slumped and that of public service unions like NALGO and NUPE increased. The union movement became more of a white-collar than a manual workers' movement. Even more significant than this internal shift in the balance of power, perhaps, was the absolute decline in trade union membership which occurred in the course of the 1980s. In 1979 there were 13.3 million trade unionists, representing 55.4 per cent of the workforce. By 1989 the figure had fallen to 10.2 million, a density of 39 per cent. The fall was explained partly by high levels of unemployment in the mid-1980s, and by the fact that employment in older, more heavily unionised industries, and in manufacturing generally, was shrinking. The new service industries which were the growth area of the 1980s were resistant to union penetration. The government's union reforms may have had some impact here; the increasing number of small businesses, and of self-employed and part-time workers, also contributed to the 'de-unionisation' of the labour market.

Changing membership patterns and an overall decline in strength affected the outlook of the trade unions and the ways in which they sought to protect the interests of their members. The failure of the miners' strike of 1984–5 was a final throwback to the days when trade union struggles were seen as an extension of the class war. By the end of the 1980s a significantly different philosophy had come to prevail. To some extent this was a function of the 'professionalisation' both of union membership and of trade union leaders.[36] The growth of middle class trade unionism, among teachers, university lecturers and others, had made it increasingly difficult to sustain the image of the unions as purely working class organisations in any meaningful sense of the term. On top of that, the economic climate of the 1980s and the lowering of expectations about what unions could achieve had imposed a 'new realism' on union leaders. This implied a willingness to moderate pay settlements, to alter working practices in order to preserve jobs and maintain company profitability, and a readiness to consider alternatives to existing bargaining structures. The negotiation of some single-union, no-strike deals, though not officially favoured by the TUC, was one example of the way in which the unions were adapting to the times.[37] Although the big disputes of the 1980s hit the headlines in Britain and abroad, the underlying reality was of a more flexible, businesslike trade unionism than in the previous two decades, a reversion in some respects to the 'Bevinism' of the 1930s rather than the extreme sectionalism of the 1970s. These changes were reflected in the fall in the number of industrial disputes in the late 1980s, even if these figures were also influenced by the return of rising unemployment after 1988. In 1990 there were only 611 official strikes in Britain, leading to no more than 1.8 million working days being lost, the lowest total for over half a century.[38]

The more sober mood of the 1980s eventually had its effect on the Labour party as well. Following the defeat of 1979 the party engaged in a prolonged spasm of self-destruction. When James Callaghan resigned the leadership in 1980 he was succeeded by the amiable radical, Michael Foot. Foot had been elected by Labour MPs to hold the party together, but proved unable to do so. The party's left, led by Tony Benn, were temporarily in the ascendant, and used the aftermath of electoral defeat to force a number of constitutional and policy changes on the party leadership, including an electoral college of trade unions, constituency parties and MPs for electing the party leader, the compulsory re-selection of MPs in each parliament and support for unilateral nuclear disarmament, a cause sympathetic to Michael Foot but not to the party's right wing or to a majority of Labour voters. The immediate result, in the spring of 1981, was the resignation from the party of more than twenty Labour MPs and other prominent figures (including the 'Gang of Four' – David Owen, Shirley Williams, William Rodgers and Roy Jenkins) to found the Social Democratic Party. The SDP flourished briefly in alliance with the Liberals, Shirley Williams and Roy Jenkins winning seats in parliament for Crosby and Glasgow Hillhead respectively at by-elections. Labour meanwhile indulged in a further bout of fratricidal strife which Foot's leadership was unable to check. When Mrs Thatcher called a general election for June 1983 Labour was ill-prepared and fared badly. It received only 27.6 per cent of the popular vote (compared with 36.9 per cent at its previous defeat in 1979) and was only narrowly ahead of the 7.7 million votes cast for the Alliance parties. Labour retained 209 seats to the Alliance's 23, but the Conservatives swept to a landslide victory, with a majority of 144.[39]

The 1983 result intensified speculation that the Labour party was entering a period of terminal decline. One particularly striking fact was the extent to which its support had been eroded even among working class and trade union voters. In 1983 Labour received the votes of 32 per cent of skilled workers and 41 per cent of unskilled workers, as against 41 per cent and 49 per cent of these categories in 1979. Among trade unionists, Labour's support had fallen from 51 per cent in 1979 to 29 per cent in 1983, actually a smaller proportion than the 31 per cent who voted Conservative.[40] The inescapable conclusion, much discussed by commentators, was that the Labour party was suffering not only from the contraction of the manual working class, but also that the internal squabbles and policy shifts of the early 1980s had antagonised a substantial proportion of those of the party's traditional constituency who remained. The fact that with unemployment at record levels, a high incidence of industrial discontent and Mrs Thatcher's personal popularity on the wane the Labour party could not do better in actual elections or in the opinion polls was a bird of bad omen for its uncertain future.

Even so, the obituaries for the party were premature. Labour's residual strength remained considerable. Under a dynamic new leader, Neil Kinnock, the excesses of the early 1980s were brought more firmly under control. The activities of the Marxist 'Militant Tendency' on Merseyside were the subject of purges and expulsions; a Bennite challenge for the leadership was beaten off; new, more centrist, policies were adopted on defence and the economy to appeal to middle class voters who had supported the Alliance in 1983 and the 'Thatcherite' working class who had voted Conservative. At the election of 1987 Labour's share of the vote increased to 30.8 per cent and it won twenty more seats than in 1983. The Conservatives retained an overall majority of a hundred seats, but there was some comfort for Labour in the faltering of the Alliance, which polled 23.6 per cent of the vote and returned 22 MPs. More than that, the SDP and Liberal parties were plunged into immediate turmoil by proposals for merger which were fiercely resisted by the Owenite minority in the SDP. Not until 1989–90 did the merged 'Liberal Democrats', led by Paddy Ashdown, begin to make electoral ground again, and by then they had fallen well behind Neil Kinnock's 'New Model' Labour party in the polls. With the replacement of Margaret Thatcher as Prime Minister by John Major in the autumn of 1990 all three parties were competing for the centre ground, but Labour was at least fighting as one of the two major parties and a serious contender for government, which it had not been in either 1983 or 1987.

The balance sheet of the Thatcher years showed a record of mixed achievements for the Conservatives on both the political and industrial fronts. Decisive victories had been registered over Labour in three successive general elections, helped by the electoral system and by the upsurge of the Alliance which had split the anti-Conservative vote. The incidence of strikes had been reduced to a fifty-year low; the problems of 'union power' were little more than a memory, at least by the end of the decade. There were signs that politicians and industrial leaders on all sides accepted the 'enterprise consensus' and that nationalisation as a means of organising a mixed economy was a dead letter. There had been significant changes in working practices and in industrial attitudes. On the other hand, Britain's underlying economic problems had not been solved. Unemployment came down in the third quarter of the 1980s, yet by the end of 1990 it was climbing steeply once more. A large trade deficit and a negative rate of economic growth were not hopeful signs for the future. Poverty, low pay and underemployment remained serious structural problems, as they had been a century before. A disaffected underclass of the poor and the deprived was permanently excluded from the benefits of 'Thatcherism', while government reforms in the health service and local government (most notoriously, the ill-fated community charge or 'poll tax') had aroused more general electoral unease and had enabled the Labour party to rebuild its platform around a promise to defend the welfare state, the one component of the post-war consensus which retained widespread respect and allegiance. Mrs Thatcher may have come as close as any Prime Minister since Stanley Baldwin to solving the Labour question as a problem in British politics. The rewards for the community were, at best, delayed.

CONCLUSION

It may still be too early to make balanced historical judgements about the 1980s, but some broad conclusions can be offered in relation to the themes treated in the period since 1868 as a whole. It has been shown that, from the 1860s on, 'labour' questions of various kinds occupied a place of increasing importance in political debate. Discussion of the improvement of conditions through the extension of state regulation was followed by interventionist measures of welfare reform to relieve the consequences of unemployment and later by the application of more sophisticated theories of economic management. As early as the 1880s, consideration of the Labour question was bound up with the debate about Britain's economic decline, as industrialists and politicians sought ways of improving efficiency and raising industrial performance. In the post-1945 period, agreement with the trade unions was seen as essential to the maintenance of a direct relationship between pay and productivity, while the Thatcher government after 1979 revived the idea widely aired at the turn of the century that it was trade union restrictive practices which prevented the implementation of the more flexible working arrangements that were necessary to create faster economic growth. Economic factors were already important in determining the outcome of elections in the 1870s; a century later they had become fundamental to success or failure at the polls.

As the organised Labour movement grew in strength, politicians had to find ways of accommodating it within the industrial and political structures of the day. The mid-Victorian settlement provided a comprehensive solution to this problem in the 1870s, granting legal rights to the trade unions of skilled workers and accepting the lobbying function of the TUC as a representative outlet for Labour views. The assimilation of Labour was made easier by the basically co-operative attitude of mid-Victorian trade unionists and their readiness, even eagerness, to work with employers to ensure the prosperity of their industries. By the late-nineteenth and early-twentieth centuries, however, the stability of this system was under threat, both from the growth of a new, more militant, mass trade unionism and from a strengthening anti-union hostility in the form of the employers' counterattack. In trying to redraw the mid-Victorian settlement, the Liberal government of Campbell-Bannerman extended trade union immunities and placed the trade unions, in one sense, outside the law. At the same time, although the voluntary system of industrial relations was upheld, and ideas of compulsory arbitration were rejected, the state became more involved in the work of industrial conciliation and in 'holding the ring' between capital and labour. In the period of sustained industrial unrest from 1910 to 1926, in which revolutionary and syndicalist ideas were at work in the trade union movement, there were times when organised Labour seemed to threaten the existence of the state itself. The government response was seen in the form of high-profile policing of strikes and the use of troops and the intelligence services to monitor and contain discontent. Revolution was perhaps never a real possibility in the 'flashpoints' of 1910–13, 1919–21 or during the General Strike of 1926, but the temporary alienation of organised Labour from the state was the result, a process consolidated by the experience of depression and mass unemployment in the 1930s.

The long-term political response to this alienation of Labour was the development of some form of corporate approach to industrial problems. There were hesitant efforts in this direction before 1914 with the setting up of the Industrial Council. During the First World War, Labour became closely associated with the organisation of war production and there was an attempt to continue this liaison into the period of peacetime, via the Whitley Councils and the National Industrial Conference. Yet, despite the establishment of joint industrial councils in many industries, and growing co-operation between unions and employers (for example in the Mond-Turner talks of 1928–9), a tripartite corporate relationship had not really been cemented prior to the outbreak of the Second World War, notwithstanding the work of Steel-Maitland as Minster of Labour in the 1920s and the experiment of the Economic Advisory Council during MacDonald's second government. From the 1940s to the 1970s, though, a more corporate pattern of relations between employers, unions and the state did evolve. The unions were partially integrated into the machinery of government during the war. Thereafter the relationship was more associative, through bodies such as the NEDC, but under both Labour and Conservative governments the unions were regularly consulted about industrial and economic policy and the TUC made formal and informal arrangements with ministers on their behalf.

However, the corporate relationship had its drawbacks and limitations. To its critics outside the unions its main disadvantage was that it gave the unions too big a say in determining policy. To those inside the unions, the main objection was that it weakened trade union independence and so could actually operate against the workers' interests. This last view underlay the unofficial rank-and-file revolts that punctuated government-union relations from the 1940s onwards. They flared up in illegal strikes during the war itself; in the 1960s and 1970s they took the form of the shop stewards' campaign for plant-based bargaining in preference to nationally agreed pay policies. Corporatism was thus effectively self-defeating, not because the unions dictated policy to the government, as the right-wing critics claimed, but rather because by aligning themselves with a policy of pay restraint the union leaders undermined their own authority within the wider trade union movement. Nevertheless, the critics were correct insofar as they argued that 'union power' was economically disruptive. For a time, especially in the 1970s, the combination of strong unions and weak governments produced a situation in which Britain was, industrially speaking, virtually ungovernable. Corporatism contributed to the dilemma but was unable to resolve it. Nor did legislative action alone provide the answer, as the Donovan Commission warned and the Heath government discovered to its painful cost. It was not so much the specific reforms of the Thatcher administration which reversed the situation as the general determination of the government to end the era of 'beer and sandwiches at Number Ten' and to keep the unions at arm's length in the formulation of policy. Possibly the anti-corporatist pendulum has now swung too far, though the likely result in the end will be a new equilibrium closer to the model of the 1870s than the 1970s, with unions having access to ministers and membership of some government committees, but with their rights and responsibilities more clearly defined in law than under the Trades Disputes Acts of 1906 or 1946. In this reversion, the weakening of the unions by mass unemployment, the pressure of public opinion and the actions of Conservative governments in the 1980s will all have played their part.

What, finally, of the political or electoral dimension of the Labour question and its effect on the industrial history of the twentieth century? We have seen that the growing electoral power of the organised working class and the emergence of a separate Labour party before 1914 challenged the political duopoly of the Liberal and Conservative parties. Both parties reacted to the challenge by pursuing what have been described as 'strategies of integration' designed to prevent a fatally damaging transition to a purely class-based system of politics. The Conservatives offered Chamberlainite imperialism mixed with promises of material prosperity through tariff reform. The Liberals provided social welfare in the form of the New Liberalism. Each, in their own way, stressed the importance of class collaboration rather than class conflict and the need for capital and labour to work together in the national and community interest.

The First World War broke the pattern of British politics. It led to the creation of a coalition government of 'national efficiency', including the Labour party, but this arrangement did not survive the war. After 1918 the Labour party moved firmly away from the tutelage of the pre-war progressive alliance and the wartime coalition and became a contender for power in its own right. With the rapid decline of the independent Liberal party, the politics of the 1920s seemed to become an industrial contest of the kind that Edwardian politicians had feared, with the 'businessmen's governments' of Lloyd George, Bonar Law and Baldwin on the one side and a Labour party heavily dependent on the trade unions on the other. It was as if the 'Labour question' had been made into the sole dividing line of political allegiance. Yet this phase of party politics was short-lived, at least in the sense that the Labour party under Ramsay MacDonald was more than the expression of trade union interests. By 1945, Attlee's Labour party was a broadly based social democratic party of which the trade unions were one, but only one, component. Even then, as psephological surveys of every period since the 1860s have shown, there was always a substantial minority of trade unionists whose individual allegiance was in the Conservative, or for that matter, the Liberal, camp.

In fact, the Labour party, when in government, suffered as much as, if not more than, the Conservatives from 'labour' problems. Like the Liberals before them, their special status as the 'friends' of the trade unions could place them in a difficult and contradictory dilemma. On the one hand, they were committed, out of loyalty and electoral self-interest, to enacting measures for the unions' benefit. Yet they also had a responsibility to other sections of the community and to their non-union, non-working class voters. In the 1890s and 1900s the Liberals felt this dilemma most acutely in the area of industrial relations and in particular the maintenance of order during industrial disputes. The New Liberalism was predicated upon assumptions of the compatibility and reconcilability of capital and labour, but this of necessity placed Liberal politicians above the industrial struggle, as referees rather than protagonists. In their turn, Labour politicians found themselves in a similar pre-dicament when they decided, in the 1960s, to attempt to restrain industrial conflict. This was the origin of the controversy over *In Place of Strife*; it led to the 'winter of discontent' and the downfall of the Callaghan government, just as the Conservatives' more straightforward resistance to the unions led to the downfall of Heath and the execration of Thatcher.

What impact has this industrialisation of politics had, not just on the party system but upon the government of the country and the performance of the economy? The ideologists of the centre in recent years have claimed that a political system which institutionalises industrial conflict in the structure of parties is inherently bad and has contributed in no small measure to Britain's economic decline. This is not the place to enlarge on the wider theme of the nation's economic shortcomings. It may be that a system of alternating, two-party government has led to some instability in policy-making, for example over the virtues of nationalisation or the desirability of an incomes policy. Yet the fact remains that for thirty years after 1945 a fair degree of consensus was preserved, regardless of the party composition of the government. Industrial discontent was as serious under Labour as under Conservative administrations. Of course, it is impossible to tell how far industrial attitudes were moulded by adversarial politics, or *vice versa*. But it is difficult to believe that the party system itself has contributed to economic weakness, if only because it is not based on industrial divisions to the extent that some analyses have claimed. What has really been at issue is not so much the differences between parties, as the divide between politicians of all parties and the 'governing institutions' of industry (to use Middlemas's phrase) and their members, employers and unions alike. In the mid-Victorian period a settlement based on an agreed division of responsibility and a shared consensus of goals provided a measure of stability and national prosperity without tending to institutional corporatism or irreconcilable conflict. As government retreats from the day to day management of the economy and of industrial relations, and as the unions revert to a more industrial and less political role (with the TUC as lobbyist on the 1870s model), perhaps a new era of 'social partnership' will permit the restoration of stability and arrest the downward curve of industrial decline.

Appendix 1
Chronology

1868	First meeting of TUC; Gladstone's first ministry.
1869	Royal Commission on Trade Unions report.
1871	Trade Union Act; Criminal Law Amendment Act. TUC Parliamentary Committee established.
1874	General election: two Lib-Lab MPs elected. Disraeli PM.
1875	Conspiracy and Protection of Property Act; Employer and Workmen Act.
1880	Gladstone's second ministry; Employers' Liability Act.
1885	Royal Commission on the Depression in Trade and Industry. General election: eleven Lib-Lab MPs returned.
1886	Gladstone's third ministry: Henry Broadhurst appointed under secretary at the Home Office. SDF demonstrations of unemployed; West End riots; 'Chamberlain circular'. Liberal split over Irish Home Rule. Labour Electoral Association set up by TUC.
1888	Mid-Lanark by-election.
1889	London dock strike: 'new unionism'.
1892	Keir Hardie elected MP for South West Ham.
1893	Independent Labour Party founded. Labour Department established at Board of Trade. Rosebery's intervention in coal dispute.
1896	Conciliation Act
1897–8	Engineering lock out: 'employers' counterattack'.
1900	Labour Representation Committee formed.
1901	Taff Vale Judgement
1903	Gladstone-MacDonald pact.
1906	General election: Liberal landslide; 29 LRC MPs form 'Labour party'. Trade Disputes Act.
1909	Osborne Judgement. Affiliation of MFGB to Labour party.

153

1910–14	Widespread industrial unrest; spread of Syndicalism. National Insurance Act (1911); Trade Union Act (1913).
1915	Treasury Agreement. Labour joins Asquith coalition.
1916	Lloyd George coalition. Arthur Henderson in War Cabinet. Ministry of Labour established.
1918	'Coupon election'. Labour the main opposition party.
1919–22	Industrial unrest. National Industrial Conference (1919). Sankey Commission on coal industry. 'Black Friday' (1921). TUC 'General Council'. TGWU formed.
1922	Fall of Lloyd George Coalition. General election – 142 Labour MPs elected.
1924	First Labour government.
1926	General Strike.
1927	Trades Disputes and Trade Union Act.
1928	Mond-Turner talks.
1929–31	Second Labour government. Formation of National Government (1931); Labour party reduced to 46 MPs at 1931 election.
1936	Jarrow March.
1940	Labour joins Churchill coalition; Ernest Bevin Minister of Labour and National Service.
1942	Beveridge Report.
1944	White Paper on Employment.
1945	General election; first majority Labour government, Clement Attlee Prime Minister.
1946–9	Nationalisation of coal, railways, gas and electricity. National Health Service and National Insurance Acts.
1951	Labour defeated in general election; return of Conservative government under Winston Churchill.
1960	Labour party Scarborough conference.
1962	Trade unions join National Economic Development Council.
1964	Harold Wilson forms Labour government.
1966	General election: Labour majority increased. National seamen's strike; Prices and Incomes Act; Frank Cousins resigns from government.
1968	Report of Donovan Commission.
1969	*In Place of Strife*. Industrial Relations Bill abandoned after TUC protest.
1970	General election: formation of Heath government.

1971	Industrial Relations Act established National Industrial Relations Court.
1972	Miners' strike; State of Emergency declared. Government introduces pay policy.
1973	Oil price rise. Miners' overtime ban. Britain enters EEC.
1974	February general election: Heath government defeated, Harold Wilson returns as Labour PM. Second general election in October.
1975	Margaret Thatcher elected leader of Conservative party. Anti-inflation policy agreed between government and TUC as part of 'social contract'. National Enterprise Board created.
1976	James Callaghan succeeds Wilson as PM.
1977	Firemen's strike. TUC votes to return to free collective bargaining.
1978–9	'Winter of discontent'.
1979	Labour government defeated in vote of confidence. General election won by Conservatives, Margaret Thatcher PM.
1980	National steel strike. Employment Act begins programme of trade union reform.
1983	General election: Conservative landslide.
1984–5	Miners' strike.
	Programme of privatisation.
1987	Conservatives re-elected for third term.
1990	John Major succeeds Margaret Thatcher as PM.

APPENDIX 2
TRADE UNION MEMBERSHIP AND THE LABOUR VOTE

	Trade Union Membership	*Labour Vote*
1895	1,530,000	
1900	2,022,000	62,698*
1906	2,210,000	321,663
1910	2,565,000	505,657 (J)
		371,802 (D)
1918	6,533,000	2,245,777
1922	5,625,000	4,237,349
1923	5,429,000	4,439,780
1924	5,544,000	5,489,087
1929	4,858,000	8,370,417
1931	4,624,000	6,649,630
1935	4,867,000	8,325,491
1945	7,875,000	11,967,746
1950	9,289,000	13,266,176
1951	9 535,000	13,948,883
1955	9,741,000	12,405,254
1959	9,632,000	12,216,172
1964	10,218,000	12,205,508
1966	10,262,000	13,096,629
1970	11,179,000	12,208,758
1974	11,755,000	11,645,616 (F)
		11,457,079 (O)
1979	13,300,000	11,532,148
1983	11,200,000	8,456,504
1987	10,500,000	10,029,270

*Figures before 1918 for LRC/Labour Party candidates only

NOTES

INTRODUCTION

1. Quoted in P. Ziegler, *Melbourne* (London, 1976), p. 158.
2. It is admittedly controversial to talk about Labour as an organised interest group in this period. It is also important to note that at this time much support for measures of labour reform came from Tories rather than Whigs.

1   THE EMERGENCE OF THE LABOUR QUESTION, 1868–1906

1. The 'new model' label was applied by Sidney and Beatrice Webb in their classic *History of Trade Unionism* (London, 1920).
2. Henry Phelps Brown, *The Origins of Trade Union Power* (Oxford, 1986), pp. 23–9.
3. John Morley, *Life of Gladstone* (London, 1908), vol. 1, p. 569.
4. In Hornby v Close the Bradford branch of the Boilermakers Society were prevented from recovering funds embezzled by their treasurer because the judges ruled that they were not governed by the terms of the 1855 Friendly Societies Act and therefore had no status in law.
5. The other members of the 'Junta' were William Allan, George Odger, Edward Coulson and Daniel Guile.
6. Ross Martin, *TUC: The Growth of a Pressure Group, 1868–1976* (Oxford, 1980), p. vii.
7. W. H. G. Armytage, *A. J. Mundella, 1825–1897. The Liberal Background to the Labour Movement* (London, 1951).
8. Quoted in Samuel H. Beer, *Modern British Politics* (London, 1966), p. 264. For a full study of the reforms of the Disraeli government see, Paul Smith, *Disraelian Conservatism and Social Reform* (London, 1967).

9. Peter Mathias, *The First Industrial Nation* (2nd edn, London, 1983), chapter 15.

10. M. E. Rose, *The Relief of Poverty, 1834–1914* (London, 1972), gives a good general treatment of this theme.

11. The subtitle of his book was 'An Inquiry into the Causes of Industrial Depression and of Increase of Want with Increase of Wealth'.

12. Memorandum, quoted in Stephen Gwynn and Gertrude Tuckwell, *The Life of Sir Charles Dilke* (London, 1917), vol. 2, p. 21.

13. José Harris, *Unemployment and Politics* (Oxford, 1972) is the basic text for the study of unemployment policy before 1914.

14. *The Times*, 9 February 1886.

15. For a list of general texts on trade union history, see the bibliographical essay below.

16. *TUC Annual Report, 1887*

17. Viscount Samuel, *Memoirs* (London, 1945), p. 6.

18. Roger Davidson, *Whitehall and the Labour Problem in Late-Victorian and Edwardian Britain* (London, 1985), pp. 34–5.

19. P. J. Macdonell, 'The Historic Basis of Liberalism, in *Essays in Liberalism by Six Oxford Men* (London, 1897), p. 261.

20. E. H. Hunt, *British Labour History, 1815–1914* (London, 1981), p. 319.

21. Harris, *Unemployment and Politics*, pp. 75–6.

22. *Ibid.*, p. 75.

23. *Ibid.*, pp. 157–65, 168–80.

24. David Powell, 'The Liberal Ministries and Labour, 1892–1895', *History*, October, 1983, pp. 408–26.

25. Davidson, *Labour Problem*, is the fullest analysis of the history of the Labour Department. See also the same author's 'Llewellyn Smith, the Labour Department and government growth' in Gillian Sutherland (ed.), *Studies in the Growth of Nineteenth-century Government* (London, 1972), pp. 227–62.

26. It should be pointed out, however, that it was only from the 1890s that reliable records were kept. Even then, the 30.4 million days lost in 1893 was exceptional, not exceeded until 1912. Henry Pelling, *A History of British Trade Unionism* (3rd edn, London, 1976), pp. 293–4.

27. John Saville, 'Trade Unions and Free Labour: the background to the Taff Vale Decision', in Asa Briggs and John Saville (eds), *Essays in Labour History* (London, 1960), pp. 328–30.

28. Roger Geary, *Policing Industrial Disputes, 1893–1985* (London,

1986), chapter 2, provides a balanced recent analysis of the Featherstone case.

29.   Roger Davidson, 'Social Conflict and Social Administration: The Conciliation Act in British Industrial Relations', in T. C. Smout (ed.), *The Search for Wealth and Stability* (London, 1979) chapter 9.

30.   This was argued by L. G. C. Money, *Riches and Poverty* (London, 1905).

31.   Viscount Gladstone Papers, BL Add MSS 45988, ff. 101–2.

32.   For general studies of the New Liberalism see Michael Freeden, *The New Liberalism* (Oxford, 1978) and Peter Clarke, *Liberals and Social Democrats* (Cambridge, 1978). On Hobhouse, Stefan Collini, *Liberalism and Sociology* (Cambridge, 1979) is valuable. See also, David Powell, 'The New Liberalism and the Rise of Labour, 1886–1906' *Historical Journal*, June 1986, pp. 369–93.

33.   James Mawdsley of the Cotton Spinners was a 'Con-Lab' candidate in the Oldham by-election of 1899. On Lancashire generally, see Patrick Joyce, *Work, Society and Politics* (London, 1982). Martin Pugh, *The Tories and the People* (Blackwell, Oxford, 1985) offers a study of popular Conservatism through the prism of the Primrose League.

34.   A full account of the dispute is contained in R. Mervyn Jones, *The North Wales Quarrymen, 1874–1922* (Cardiff, 1982).

35.   E. W. Evans, *Mabon* (Cardiff, 1959), p. 38.

36.   Henry Pelling, *Origins of the Labour Party* (Oxford, 1965), p. 116.

37.   *Ibid.*, pp. 13–37.

38.   The socialist element in the new party was weakened by the withdrawal of the SDF from the LRC in 1901.

39.   Henry Pelling, *A Short History of the Labour Party* (London, 1976), p. 4.

40.   Peter Clarke, 'The Progressive Movement in England', *Transactions of the Royal Historical Society*, 1974, pp. 159–81; *Lancashire and the New Liberalism* (Cambridge, 1971).

41.   Memorandum by Jesse Herbert, Viscount Gladstone Papers, BL Add MSS 46025, f. 131.

42.   Powell, 'New Liberalism'; Freeden, *New Liberalism*, pp. 123–8.

2 THE LIBERAL MINISTRIES AND LABOUR, 1906–15

1. A. K. Russell, *Liberal Landslide* (Newton Abbot, 1973), p. 79.
2. John Wilson, *CB. A Life of Sir Henry Campbell-Bannerman* (London, 1973), pp. 504–5.
3. For a fuller consideration of the 1906 Act, see Phelps Brown *Origins of Trade Union Power*, pp. 32–59.
4. On the pre-war unrest, see James Hinton, *Labour and Socialism* (Brighton, 1983), pp. 83–95; Henry Pelling, 'The Labour Unrest 1911–14' in his *Popular Politics and Society in Late-Victorian Britain* (2nd edn, London, 1979), pp. 147–64.
5. A good general account of the economic background is T. R. Gourvish, 'The Standard of Living, 1890–1914' in Alan O'Day (ed.), *The Edwardian Age* (London, 1979), pp. 13–33.
6. Pelling, *British Trade Unionism*, p. 293.
7. C. J. Wrigley, *David Lloyd George and the British Labour Movement* (Brighton, 1976).
8. *Ibid.*, Chapter III.
9. G. R. Askwith, *Industrial Problems and Disputes* (London, 1920).
10. For full statements of their views, see J. A. Hobson, *The Crisis of Liberalism* (London, 1909), L. T. Hobhouse, *Liberalism* (London, 1911). Also important in the debate were individual reformers like Seebohm Rowntree and the writers and journalists of the *Nation* group, whose meetings were organised by H. W. Massingham. Clarke, *Liberals and Social Democrats* provides the context. For background, see also J. R. Hay, *The Origins of the Liberal Welfare Reforms* (London, 1975).
11. Churchill's letter to *The Nation* ('The Untrodden Field') is quoted in Kenneth O. Morgan, *The Age of Lloyd George* (London, 1971), pp. 144–8.
12. For the work of the Labour Department, see the works by Davidson, cited above.
13. Speech, Cardiff, 11 October 1906, quoted in H. Du Parcq, *Life of David Lloyd George* (London, 1914), vol. iv, pp. 630–1.
14. The sliding scale committees were so called because they determined the level of wages in relation to the price of coal.
15. K. D. Brown, *Labour and Unemployment, 1900–1914* (Newton Abbot, 1971).
16. On Beveridge, the basic text is José Harris, *William Beveridge*

(Oxford, 1977). See also the same author's *Unemployment and Politics*.

17.   For example, Campbell-Bannerman to Herbert Gladstone, 2 January 1905, Viscount Gladstone Papers, BL Add MSS 45988, f. 140.

18.   Martin Pugh, *Lloyd George* (London, 1988), pp. 30–7.

19.   *Ibid.*, pp. 42–5, 63–6.

20.   Jane Ridley, 'The Unionist Social Reform Committee, 1911–1914', *Historical Journal*, 1987, pp. 391–413.

21.   The point is amplified in Henry Pelling, 'The Working Class and the Origins of the Welfare State', in *Popular Politics and Society*, pp. 1–18, and Pat Thane, 'The Working Class and State "Welfare" in Britain, 1880–1914', *Historical Journal*, 1984, pp. 877–900. Keith Burgess, *The Challenge of Labour* (London, 1980), pp. 122–33, provides a devastating critique of some of the limitations of the New Liberalism.

22.   Keith Laybourn, *The Rise of Labour* (London, 1988) is a good historiographical summary. The 'progressivist' case is set out in the works of Peter Clarke cited in Ch. 1. For the alternative view, see, Ross McKibbin, *The Evolution of the Labour Party, 1910–1924* (Oxford, 1974) and some of the essays in K. D. Brown (ed.), *The First Labour Party, 1906–14* (London, 1985). Duncan Tanner, *Political Change and the Labour Party, 1900–1918* (Cambridge, 1990) is the fullest study of 'progressive' politics, but see also Martin Petter, 'The Progressive Alliance', *History*, 1973, pp. 45–59.

23.   Martin Pugh, *The Making of Modern British Politics, 1867–1939* (Blackwell, Oxford, 1982), pp. 137–41.

24.   F. W. S. Craig, *British Electoral Facts, 1885–1975* (London, 1976), pp. 7–8. (The percentages are for share of the national vote. In constituencies contested it was obviously in most cases considerably higher, averaging 36.6 per cent in January and 40.88 per cent in December. McKibbin, *The Evolution of the Labour Party, 1910–1924*, p. 16) The most complete study of the 1910 elections is Neal Blewett, *The Peers, the Parties and the People* (London, 1972).

25.   In 1906 the miners had formed the bulk of the 24-strong Lib-Lab group.

26.   Pugh, *Modern British Politics*, p. 139.

27.   Roy Douglas, 'Labour in Decline', in K. D. Brown (ed.), *Essays in Anti-Labour History* (London, 1974), pp. 105–25. Two seats were lost to the Conservatives, two to the Liberals.

28. H. C. G. Matthew, R. I. McKibbin and J. A. Kay, 'The Franchise Factor in the Rise of the Labour Party', *English Historical Review*, 1976, pp. 723–52; Duncan Tanner, 'The Parliamentary Electoral System, the 'Fourth' Reform Act and the Rise of Labour in England and Wales', *Bulletin of the Institute of Historical Research*, 1983, pp. 205–19; P. F. Clarke, 'Liberals, Labour and the Franchise', *English Historical Review*, 1977, pp. 582–9.

29. Pugh, *Modern British Politics*, p. 149. Michael Cahill, 'Labour in the Municipalities' in K. D. Brown (ed.), *The First Labour Party*, pp. 89–104.

30. McKibbin, *Evolution of the Labour Party*, pp. 72–87.

31. Alun Howkins, 'Edwardian Liberalism and Industrial Unrest', *History Workshop Journal*, 1977, pp. 143–61.

32. Laybourn *Rise of Labour*, pp. 13–15, 26–30.

33. Arthur Marwick, *The Deluge* (2nd edn, London, 1991)

34. *The Times*, 3 March 1906.

35. The 1913 Trade Union Act had aroused considerable opposition within the Liberal party because it was seen as conceding too much to the unions and giving the Labour party an unfair political advantage.

36. Pelling, *British Trade Unionism*, pp. 149–54, examines the early stages of the war. See also Chris Wrigley, 'Trade Unions and Politics in the First World War', in Ben Pimlott and Chris Cook (eds), *Trade Unions in British Politics* (London, 1982), pp. 79–97.

37. Quoted in Pelling, *British Trade Unionism*, p. 150.

38. Full details are given in Wrigley, *Lloyd George and the Labour Movement*, pp. 91–109.

3 THE LABOUR QUESTION IN WAR AND PEACE, 1915–26

1. One estimate is that 19.5 per cent of male engineering workers had enlisted by June 1915. Burgess, *Challenge of Labour*, p. 159.

2. Wrigley, *Lloyd George and the Labour Movement* gives a good account of Lloyd George's work as Minister of Munitions, See also John Grigg, *Lloyd George From Peace to War, 1912–1916* (London, 1985).

3. Wrigley, *op. cit.*, pp. 149–63.

4. At least five ministries were involved in aspects of labour policy, namely the ministries of Labour, Munitions, Recon-

struction (from 1917), the Home Office and the Board of Trade. For an overview of wartime administration, see K. Burk (ed.), *War and the State* (London, 1982).

5. Chris Wrigley, 'Trade Unions and Politics in the First World War' in Pimlott and Cook (eds), *Trade Unions in British Politics* pp. 89–93.

6. A. J. P. Taylor, *English History 1914–1945* (Oxford, 1965), p. 132.

7. Addison's career is discussed in Kenneth and Jane Morgan, *Portrait of a Progressive* (Oxford, 1980). For the subsequent fate of these reforms, see Kenneth O. Morgan, *Consensus and Disunity: the Lloyd George Coalition Government, 1918–1922* (Oxford, 1979), Ch. 4.

8. John Sheldrake, *Industrial Relations and Politics in Britain 1880–1989* (London, 1991), pp. 29–33.

9. Pelling, *British Trade Unionism*, p. 294.

10. A good recent account of the episode is contained in Chris Wrigley, *Arthur Henderson* (Cardiff, 1990), pp. 112–19. In fairness, it should be stressed that there was more to this incident than Henderson's personal sensitivity. The issues involved reflected a deepening division between government and Labour on the question of war aims.

11. The full text of clause four is quoted in Henry Pelling, *A Short History of the Labour Party* (5th edn, London, 1976), p. 44.

12. Pugh, *Modern British Politics*, pp. 176–81; McKibbin, *Evolution of the Labour Party*, Ch. V.

13. Morgan, *Consensus and Disunity*, gives the general context. On labour questions, see also Chris Wrigley, *Lloyd George and the Challenge of Labour, 1918–1922* (Harvester, 1990).

14. Hinton, *Labour and Socialism*, p. 98.

15. For a discussion of this theme, see J. M. Winter, *The Great War and the British People* (London, 1986).

16. Alan Bullock, *The Life and Times of Ernest Bevin*, vol. 1 (London, 1960) offers a good insight into these developments.

17. This earlier period is described in E. P. Thompson, *The Making of the English Working Class* (London, 1963).

18. Morgan, *Consensus and Disunity*, Chs 3 and 4.

19. Bullock, *Ernest Bevin*, vol. 1 pp. 116–42.

20. Pelling, *British Trade Unionism*, p. 294.

21. *Ibid.*, p. 160.

22. Bullock, *Ernest Bevin*, vol. 1, pp. 143–79.

23. Pugh, *Lloyd George*, offers a general view of these questions.

See also, R. J. Scally, *The Origins of the Lloyd George Coalition: the politics of social imperialism* (Princeton, 1975); Morgan, *Consensus and Disunity*, pp. 84–5.

24. Statistics in this section are taken from F. W. S. Craig, *British Electoral Facts*, pp. 10–14.

25. The ILP candidates suffered for their earlier opposition to the war. Henderson simply suffered from an unfortunate propensity for losing seats at general elections. He repeated his 1918 misfortune in 1922, 1923 and 1931.

26. Maurice Cowling, *The Impact of Labour, 1920–1924* (Cambridge, 1971).

27. Laybourn, *The Rise of Labour*, pp. 47–66.

28. Labour also benefited from Liberal inability to contest certain seats. See Pugh, *Modern British Politics*, Chs 11 and 12, for a full discussion of electoral questions.

29. Chris Cook, *The Age of Alignment* (London, 1975), pp. 180–96.

30. *Ibid.*, Part Four, for an analysis of the election. (The Campbell case controversy arose because the Labour government discontinued the prosecution of a journalist allegedly guilty of inciting mutiny in the armed forces. The 'Zinoviev letter' was purportedly written by the head of Comintern calling on British socialists to foment a revolution. Both were exploited by the Conservatives to point out the dangers of a 'socialist' Labour government).

31. This may imply too Machiavellian a propensity on Baldwin's part. It is possible that he miscalculated in 1923 (when he almost certainly expected the Conservatives to win, albeit with a reduced majority) and that he was lucky during 1924 that events went his way. If the Liberals had done well enough in 1923 to form a minority administration of their own, things might have developed very differently.

32. The best study of the 1924 Labour government is R. Lyman, *The First Labour Government* (London, 1965). See also D. Marquand, *Ramsay MacDonald* (London, 1977), chapters 14–16.

33. Pelling, *Short History*, p. 56.

34. Bullock, *Ernest Bevin*, vol. 1, pp. 221–47.

35. For detailed accounts of the strike, see P. Renshaw, *The General Strike* (London, 1975), G. A. Phillips, *The General Strike: the Politics of Industrial Conflict* (London, 1976). There are numerous other narrative studies.

36. The negotiations are described in Bullock, *Ernest Bevin*, vol. 1, pp. 308–15.

37. *Ibid.*, pp. 333–9.
38. See Ch. 4.
39. This point is stressed in Keith Middlemas, *Politics in Industrial Society* (London, 1979), pp. 177–8, 187.
40. Quoted in Pelling, *British Trade Unionism*, p. 170.

4 DEPRESSION AND INTEGRATION, 1926–45

1.   The Lloyd George coalition had hastened the divergence by splitting the Liberal party, readmitting the Conservatives to power and driving Labour into opposition.
2.   For a discussion of the genesis and content of the Yellow Book see John Campbell, *Lloyd George: the Goat in the Wilderness* (London, 1977), pp. 183–205.
3.   Quoted in Pelling, *British Trade Unionism*, p. 187.
4.   Nearly 19 million 'anti-union' leaflets were distributed by Conservative Central Office in 1927, roughly treble the number circulated in 1926. Middlemas, *Politics in Industrial Society*, p. 202.
5.   *Ibid.*, p. 191.
6.   Bullock, *Ernest Bevin*, vol. 1, pp. 392–416.
7.   M. Beloff, *Wars and Welfare: Britain 1914–1945* (London, 1984), p. 145.
8.   D. Fraser, *The Evolution of the British Welfare State* (2nd edn, London, 1984), pp. 185–7.
9.   Campbell, *op. cit.*, pp. 225–7.
10. Craig, *British Electoral Facts*, p. 15.
11. Pelling, *Short History of the Labour Party*, p. 64.
12. See Appendix 2.
13. The best accounts of the second Labour government are in Robert Skidelsky, *Politicians and the Slump* (London, 1967) and Marquand, *Ramsay MacDonald*, Chs 21–6.
14. Campbell, *op. cit.*, Chs 9 and 10.
15. R. Mckibbin, 'The Economic Policy of the Second Labour Government 1929–1931', *Past and Present*, August 1975.
16. Marquand, *op. cit.*, Chs 25 and 26, offers an analytical narrative; an older account is R. Bassett, *1931: Political Crisis* (London, 1958).
17. Bullock, *Ernest Bevin*, vol. 1, pp. 476–91.
18. Layburn, *Rise of Labour*, pp. 67–83 provides a summary of recent literature.

19. In addition to the 46 Labour MPs, five members of the ILP were also elected.

20. The history of the NUWM is recounted in John Stevenson and Chris Cook, *The Slump: Society and Politics during the Depression* (London, 1977), pp. 145–65. This book is extremely valuable for the study of the 1930s as a whole.

21. Richard Shackleton, 'Trade Unions and the Slump' in Pimlott and Cook (eds), *Trade Unions in British Politics*, p. 120.

22. Hinton, *Labour and Socialism*, p. 120.

23. These themes are dealt with more fully in Stevenson and Cook, *op. cit.*

24. Pelling, *British Trade Unionism*, p. 295.

25. Middlemas, *Politics in Industrial Society*, p. 215.

26. Pelling, *British Trade Unionism*, p. 204.

27. Quoted, *ibid.*, p. 196.

28. Figures, *ibid.*, p. 295.

29. This example is cited as a model of good industrial relations in Bullock, *Ernest Bevin*, vol. 1, pp. 380–1.

30. Fraser, *Evolution of the Welfare State*, pp. 196–8.

31. Malcolm Smith, *British Politics, Society and the State* (London, 1990), pp. 96–8; Sydney Checkland, *British Public Policy* (Cambridge, 1983), Ch. 17.

32. Macmillan published an important book on social and industrial policy, *The Middle Way*, in 1938.

33. For Mosley's career in the 1930s, and his earlier participation in the second Labour government, see Robert Skidelsky, *Oswald Mosley* (London, 1975).

34. Middlemas, *Politics in Industrial Society*, pp. 20–1.

35. This is not to say that both employers' organisations and the TUC and its constituent unions were not trying to influence government decisions and to claim a bigger share in economic policy making.

36. Middlemas, *Politics in Industrial Society*, p. 269, quoting Paul Addison, *The Road to 1945* (London, 1975).

37. David Dutton, *British Politics Since 1945. The Rise and Fall of Consensus* (Blackwell, Oxford, 1991), pp. 9–21, provides a convenient introduction to this theme.

38. Bevin's wartime career is covered in Alan Bullock, *The Life and Times of Ernest Bevin*, vol. 2 (London, 1967), on which much of what follows is based.

39. There were only 109 prosecutions of workers under Order 1305 during the entire war. Denis Barnes and Eileen Reid, 'A

New Relationship: Trade Unions in the Second World War', in Pimlott and Cook (eds), *Trade Unions in British Politics*, p. 160.

40. In fact, there were more stoppages than in the First World War but fewer days were lost. Pelling, *British Trade Unionism*, pp. 294–5.

41. Fraser, *Evolution of the Welfare State*, pp. 214–22; Smith, *Politics, Society and the State*, pp. 160–5.

42. For a fuller discussion of this topic, see Keith Middlemas, *Power, Competition and the State*, vol. 1 (London, 1986), Ch. 2.

43. Quoted in Bullock, *Ernest Bevin*, vol. 2, pp. 305, 309.

5 BRITISH POLITICS AND THE LABOUR QUESTION SINCE 1945

1. Memories of 1918, when Lloyd George and the Conservatives had been elected but had failed to deliver their promised reforms, may also have boosted Labour support, if only at a subconscious level.

2. On the political background to the 1945 election, See Paul Addison, *The Road to 1945* (London, 1975); Henry Pelling, 'The 1945 General Election Reconsidered', *Historical Journal*, June 1980.

3. Dutton, *British Politics Since 1945*, pp. 22–40. The standard accounts of the Attlee governments are Kenneth O. Morgan, *Labour in Power, 1945–1951* (Oxford, 1984) and Henry Pelling, *The Labour Government, 1945–51* (London, 1984).

4. Arthur Marwick points out, however, that the Conservatives did force a division on the third reading of the National Health Service Bill. Marwick, *British Society Since 1945* (Penguin, 1982), p. 104.

5. Morgan, *Labour in Power*, pp. 374–7.

6. Pelling, *British Trade Unionism*, pp. 227–30.

7. The economic policies of the Labour government cannot be studied in detail here. Morgan, *Labour in Power*, contains a full account. For a briefer summary, see Alan Sked and Chris Cook, *Post-War Britain* (3rd edn, Penguin, 1990), pp. 26–38.

8. Craig, *British Electoral Facts*, pp. 21–3. Sked and Cook, *Post-War Britain*, pp. 81–6, 98–100.

9. Gallup polls in the mid-1950s confirmed declining public support for the trade unions, even among Labour voters.

10. Pelling, *Short History of the Labour Party*, pp. 105–22.

11.   Bevan had died in 1960. Wilson was one of those who had resigned with Bevan in 1951.

12.   Sked and Cook, *Post-War Britain*, pp. 217–19. (This sentence was written in September 1991).

13.   The best treatment of the Wilson governments is Clive Ponting, *Breach of Promise: Labour in Power 1964–1970* (London, 1989), although this may be supplemented by the diaries and memoirs of many of the participants.

14.   Pay policy is well covered in Robert Taylor, 'The trade union "problem" since 1960', in Pimlott and Cook (eds), *Trade Unions in British Politics*, pp. 194–208.

15.   Pelling, *British Trade Unionism*, pp. 259–60, 262.

16.   Phelps Brown, *Origins of Trade Union Power*, pp. 177–80.

17.   Quoted *ibid.*, p. 179.

18.   The Report basically upheld the existing voluntary system and warned against the dangers of trying to improve industrial relations by legislative action.

19.   Wilson may have been influenced by the pressure of public opinion as well as by his personal frustration with the unions, dating from the seamen's strike of 1966.

20.   Ponting, *Breach of Promise*, pp. 350–71.

21.   The Act was piloted through parliament by Sir Geoffrey Howe. Phelps Brown, *Trade Union Power*, Ch. XI, provides a full analysis of the Act. See also Sheldrake, *Industrial Relations and Politics*, pp. 72–6.

22.   Comparisons with the campaign against the Criminal Law Amendment Act of a century earlier are not wildly inappropriate.

23.   Geary, *Policing Industrial Disputes*, pp. 72–8.

24.   Pelling, *British Trade Unionism*, p. 283.

25.   Sked and Cook, *Post-War Britain*, pp. 285–90.

26.   *Ibid.*, p. 287.

27.   Taylor, 'The trade union "problem"', p. 204.

28.   This point is developed more fully in Robert Currie, *Industrial Politics* (Oxford, 1979), Ch. 5.

29.   Sked and Cook, *Post-War Britain*, pp. 321–2.

30.   Dutton, *British Politics Since 1945*, pp. 67, 79. Peter Thorneycroft and Enoch Powell were precursors of these views in the 1950s.

31.   Prior's successors in this post were Norman Tebbit (1981–3), Tom King (1983–5), Lord Young (1985–7), Norman Fowler (1987–90) and Michael Howard.

32. *The Times*, 25 July 1991. For a summary of the reforms and their effects see Christopher Johnson, *The Economy Under Mrs Thatcher, 1979–1990* (Penguin, 1991), Ch. 7.

33. *Ibid.*, pp. 239–45.

34. Geary, *Policing Industrial Disputes*, pp. 136–45; M. Adeney and J. Lloyd, *The Miners' Strike, 1984–5* (London, 1986).

35. E. J. Hobsbawm, *Labouring Men* (London, 1968), p. 7.

36. This theme is more fully dealt with in its wider context in Harold Perkin, *The Rise of Professional Society* (London, 1989).

37. The influence of foreign, especially Japanese, companies was important in encouraging these trends.

38. ACAS Annual Report.

39. Sked and Cook, *Post-War Britain*, p. 432.

40. A. J. Taylor, *Trade Unions and the Labour Party* (London, 1987), quoted in Laybourn, *Rise of Labour*, p. 159. It is worth noting, moreover, in the context of the debate about links between the trade unions and the Labour party, that fewer than half the unions in the TUC were affiliated to the Labour party at the beginning of the 1980s.

FURTHER READING

There are a number of studies of Trade Unionism and Labour politics which cover all or part of the period dealt with in this book. Two introductory texts by Henry Pelling, *A History of British Trade Unionism* and *A Short History of the Labour Party* (both available in recent new editions) are a good starting point. Other works on trade unionism and industrial relations are: Alan Fox, *History and Heritage: the Social Origins of the British Industrial Relations System* (London, 1985), an extremely rich and rewarding book; Ben Pimlott and Chris Cook (eds), *Trade Unions and British Politics* (2nd edn, London, 1991); Richard Price, *Labour in British Society* (London, 1985); John Sheldrake, *Industrial Relations and Politics in Britain, 1880–1989* (London, 1991) and J. Cronin, *Labour and Society, 1918–1979* (London, 1984). Some of these integrate industrial and political developments, as do James Hinton, *Labour and Socialism* (London, 1983) and Keith Burgess, *The Challenge of Labour* (London, 1980). Ross Martin, *TUC: the Growth of a Pressure Group, 1868–1976* (Oxford, 1980) offers a good survey of the development of a central institution of the Labour movement. Keith Laybourn, *The Rise of Labour. The British Labour Party, 1890–1979* (London, 1988) summarises recent historiography, while the same author's 'Readers in History' on *British Trade Unionism, 1770–1990* and *The Labour Party* (Alan Sutton, 1991 and 1988 respectively) contain selections of primary source material. One other introductory text which should be mentioned is J. Lovell, *British Trade Unions, 1875–1933* (London, 1977).

There is no study of the 'Labour question' as such, but there are two outstanding books which cover some of the same ground as the present volume in much greater depth, both factually and intellectually, namely Keith Middlemas, *Politics in Industrial Society* (London, 1979) and Robert Currie, *Industrial Politics* (Oxford, 1979). Of equal value is E. H. Phelps Brown, *The Origins of Trade Union Power* (Oxford, 1983). Broader aspects of public policy are covered

170

in Sydney Checkland, *British Public Policy, 1776–1939* (Cambridge, 1983), Derek Fraser, *The Evolution of the British Welfare State* (2nd edn, London, 1984) and Malcolm Smith, *British Society, Politics and the State* (London, 1990). An overview of the government's handling of industrial relations is provided in Roger Geary, *Policing Industrial Disputes* (London, 1985) and E. Wigham, *Strikes and the Government, 1893–1981* (London, 1982). For party politics in the period up to 1939 there is one indispensable work: Martin Pugh, *The Making of Modern British Politics, 1867–1939* (Blackwell, Oxford, 1982).

On the earlier part of the period, the best history of the Labour movement in the nineteenth century is E. H. Hunt, *British Labour History, 1815–1914* (London, 1981). Early Labour politics are considered in Royden Harrison, *Before the Socialists: Studies in Labour and Politics, 1861–1881* (London, 1965). The emergence of a separate Labour party is described in Henry Pelling, *Origins of the Labour Party* (2nd edn, Oxford, 1965) and Frank Bealey and Henry Pelling, *Labour and Politics, 1900–1906* (London, 1958). These are the standard works, but may now be supplemented by David Howell, *British Workers and the Independent Labour Party, 1888–1906* (Manchester, 1983). The 'rise of Labour' has generated a vast history. Pugh, *Modern British Politics*, and Laybourn, *Rise of Labour*, cited above, give further guidance. On the response of the Liberals, some detailed references are contained in the notes to chapter 1. One work not mentioned there but which is of use for the 1880s and 1890s is M. Barker, *Gladstone and Radicalism* (Brighton, 1975). Two biographical studies of interest are, Kenneth O. Morgan, *Keir Hardie, Radical and Socialist* (London, 1975) and David Marquand, *Ramsay MacDonald* (London, 1977), the latter of which is relevant for later periods as well.

Trade unionism, industrial relations and other aspects of labour policy in the late nineteenth and early twentieth centuries are dealt with in H. Clegg, A. Fox and A. F. Thompson, *A History of British Trade Unions since 1889*, vol. 1, *1889–1910* (Oxford, 1964) and in E. H. Phelps Brown, *The Growth of British Industrial Relations* (London, 1959). C. Wrigley (ed.), *A History of British Industrial Relations, vol 1, 1875–1914* (Brighton, 1982) is an important collection of essays by various authors. J. Harris, *Unemployment and Politics. A Study in English Social Policy, 1886–1914* (Oxford, 1972) is the most thorough treatment of its theme. Roger Davidson, *Whitehall and the Labour Problem in Late-Victorian and Edwardian Britain* (London, 1985) is a detailed investigation of the work of the Labour Department at the Board of Trade, particularly in its statistical role. These specific topics are placed in a wider context by some of the essays in M. Langan and B. Schwarz (eds), *Crises in the British State, 1880–1930* (London, 1985).

Henry Pelling's (arguably mistitled) *Popular Politics and Society in Late-Victorian Britain* (2nd edn, London, 1979) also offers stimulating views on various aspects of the Labour question in the Edwardian period. Other works which focus on the pre-1914 period and its aftermath are K. D. Brown (ed.), *The First Labour Party, 1906–1914* (London, 1985), Duncan Tanner, *Political Change and the Labour Party, 1900–1918* (Cambridge, 1990), K. Laybourn and J. Reynolds, *Liberalism and the Rise of Labour, 1890–1918* (London, 1984) and P. F. Clarke, *Lancashire and the New Liberalism* (Cambridge, 1971). The early chapters of C. J. Wrigley, *David Lloyd George and the British Labour Movement* (Brighton, 1975) discuss the industrial troubles of the pre-war years, as, from different perspectives, do B. Holton, *British Syndicalism, 1900–1914: Myth and Reality* (London, 1976), Jane Morgan, *Conflict and Order: the Police and Labour Disputes in England and Wales, 1900–1939* (Oxford, 1989) and H. A. Clegg, *A History of British Trade Unions*, vol. 2, *1910–1939* (Oxford, 1985). The best study of the pre-war Liberal reforms is probably still Bentley B. Gilbert, *The Evolution of National Insurance in Great Britain* (London, 1967).

The bibliography of the First World War and its impact on British society is large. Arthur Marwick, *The Deluge* (2nd edn, London, 1991) provides a convenient introduction, although Trevor Wilson, *The Myriad Faces of War* (Polity Press, 1986) is monumental and J. M. Winter, *The Great War and the British People* (London, 1987) is valuable for the social dimension. On Lloyd George, Wrigley's *Lloyd George and the Labour Movement*, mentioned above, is the basic text for the war period. A sequel, *Lloyd George and the Challenge of Labour* (Harvester, 1990) deals with the period after 1918. Wrigley has also edited volume two of *A History of British Industrial Relations, 1914–1939* (Brighton, 1987) and produced a brief biography of *Arthur Henderson* (Cardiff, 1990). The labour policies of the post-war coalition are analysed in Kenneth O. Morgan, *Consensus and Disunity: the Lloyd George Coalition Government, 1918–1922* (Oxford, 1979). Other important works for the immediate post-war period are Maurice Cowling, *The Impact of Labour 1920–1924* (Cambridge, 1971), a pioneering study of 'high political' responses to the rise of the Labour party, and Ross McKibbin, *The Evolution of the Labour Party, 1910–1924* (Oxford, 1974), an account of the party's organisational and policy development. R. Lyman, *The First Labour Government* (London, 1965) is probably the definitive account of its subject. On the General Strike, P. Renshaw, *The General Strike* (London, 1975) and G. A. Phillips, *The General Strike: the Politics of Industrial Conflict* (London, 1976) provide adequate coverage, although there are numerous other accounts. One biography of major importance is Alan Bullock, *The Life and Times of Ernest Bevin*, vol. 1, *1881–1940: Trade Union Leader* (London, 1960). See also R. Charles, *The Development of Industrial Relations in Britain, 1911–1939* (London, 1973).

The second Labour government is the main subject of Robert Skidelsky, *Politicians and the Slump* (London, 1967). For the 1930s. John Stevenson and Chris Cook, *The Slump* (London, 1977) is a thorough revisionist account of both economic and political aspects. The political problems of the Labour party are further explored in Ben Pimlott, *Labour and the Left in the 1930s* (Cambridge, 1977). The politics of the Second World War are dealt with in Paul Addison, *The Road to 1945* (London, 1975) and in T. Burridge, *British Labour and Hitler's War* (London, 1978). Bevin's work as Minister of Labour (and much else besides) is fully documented in volume two of Alan Bullock's biography, *Ernest Bevin, Minister of Labour* (London, 1967). A more general view of the domestic front is contained in Angus Calder, *The People's War* (London, 1969).

Bevin's injunction that the 'people's war' should be followed by *The People's Peace* has been satisfied by Kenneth O. Morgan's recent volume of that title (Oxford, 1990), which offers a polished analytical narrative of British history since 1945. Also valuable for establishing the context of the Labour question in more recent times is Alan Sked and Chris Cook, *Post-War Britain* (3rd edn, Penguin 1990). The major work on the post-1945 era, though, is the three volume study by Keith Middlemas, *Power, Competition and the State* (London, 1986, 1988, 1991), which pursues in greater depth the analysis of developing corporatism first expounded in the same author's *Politics in Industrial Society* mentioned above. One of Middlemas's themes is the erosion of the wartime consensus, a topic treated on a broader canvas in David Dutton, *British Politics Since 1945. The Rise and Fall of Consensus* (Blackwell, Historical Association, 1991). More specific works on aspects of this period have been referred to in the notes to chapter 5, but other studies which have much of relevance to say include D. Barnes and E. Reid, *Government and Trade Unions. The British Experience, 1964–1979* (London, 1980), L. Panitch, *Social Democracy and Industrial Militancy: the Labour Party, the Trade Unions and Incomes Policy, 1945–1974* (Cambridge, 1976) and A. J. Taylor, *The Trade Unions and the Labour Party* (London, 1987). A good survey of the Labour question under Thatcherism is provided by Christopher Johnson, *The Economy Under Mrs Thatcher, 1979–1990* (Penguin, 1991). For the more recent period, biographies and published diaries and memoirs can be an excellent source, albeit one of variable quality. Further guidance can be found in the bibliographies of many of the works cited.

INDEX

175

Index

Index